NEURO-DIVERSED

DONESA WALKER M. ED

WRITTEN BY: DONESA WALKER
DESIGN BY: WILL BATEN

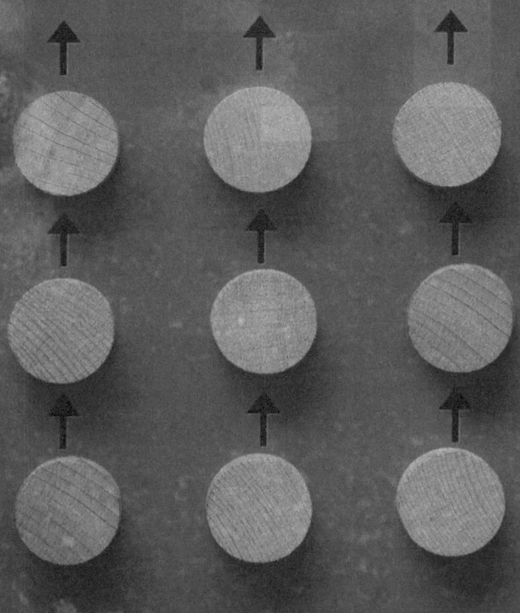

DIFFERENT IS
GOOD THEY SAY

BUT THEY AREN'T ME.

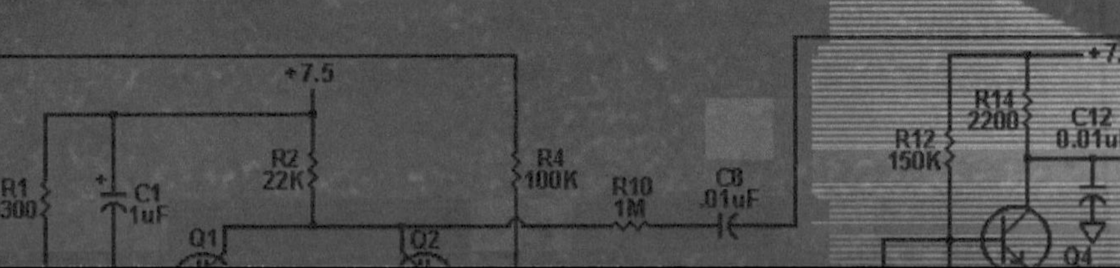

+7.5
R1 3300
C1 1uF
R2 22K
R4 100K
R10 1M
C8 .01uF
R12 150K
R14 2200
C12 0.01uF
R17 10K
+7.5
Q1
Q2

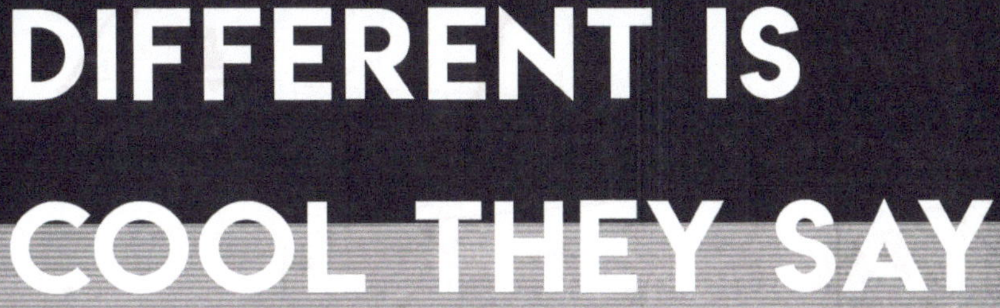

DIFFERENT IS
COOL THEY SAY

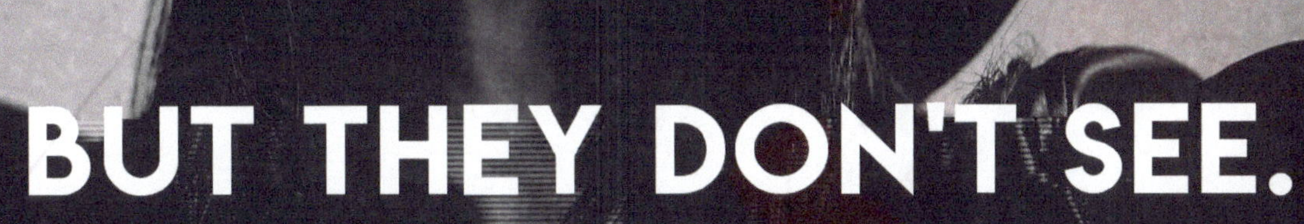

BUT THEY DON'T SEE.

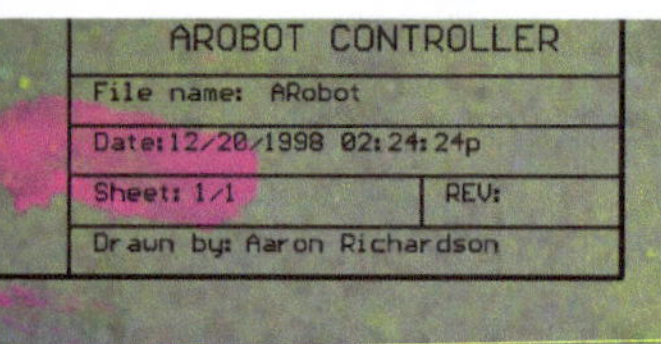

DIFFERENT IS OKAY THEY SAY BUT DON'T LET ME BE.

DIFFERENT IS FINE THEY SAY BUT I DON'T AGREE.

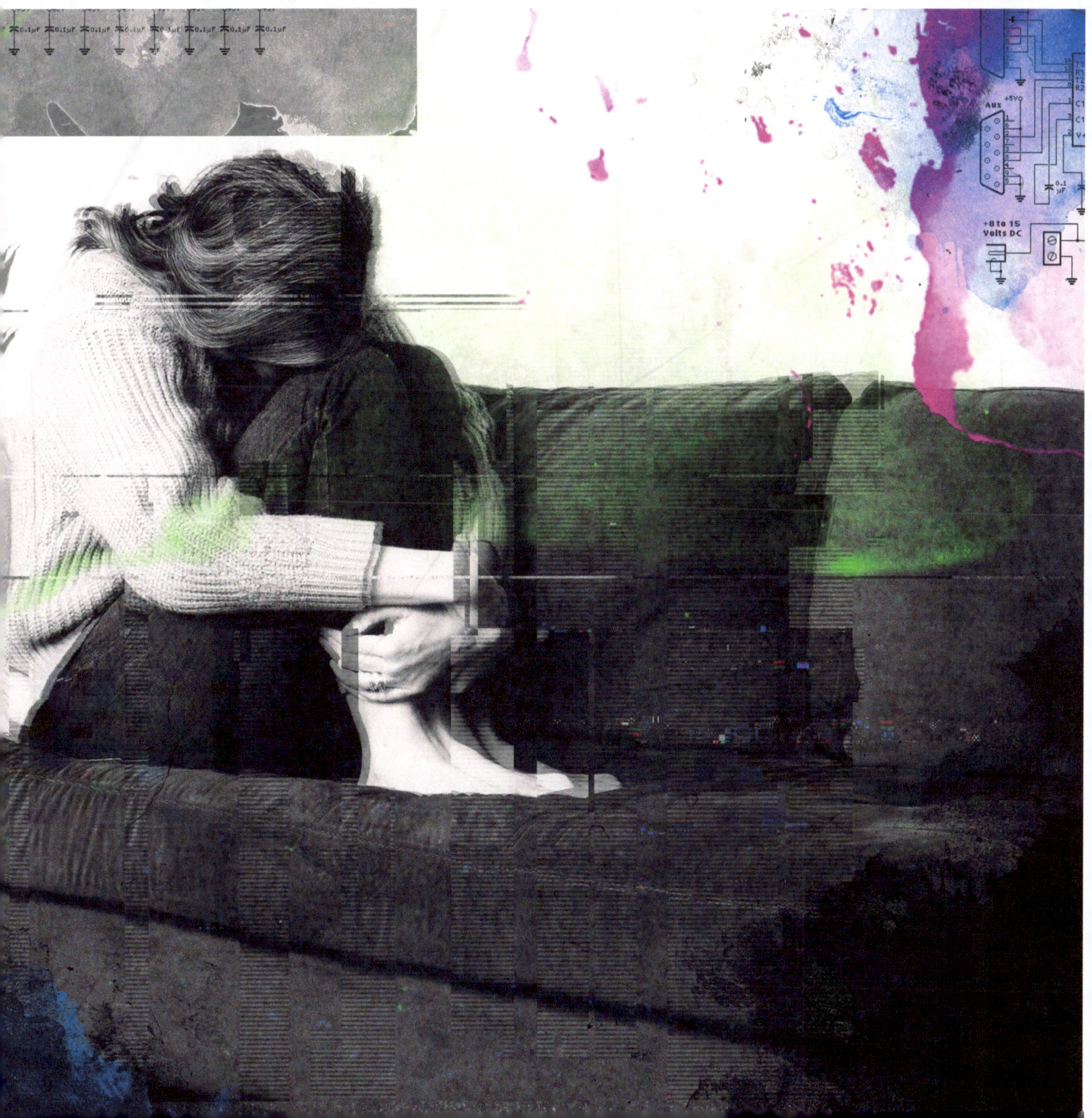
0.1μF 0.1μF 0.1μF 0.1μF 0.1μF 0.1μF 0.1μF 0.1μF
Aux +5V
+5V
R1
R2
C1
C1
V+
0.1 μF
+8 to 15
Volts DC

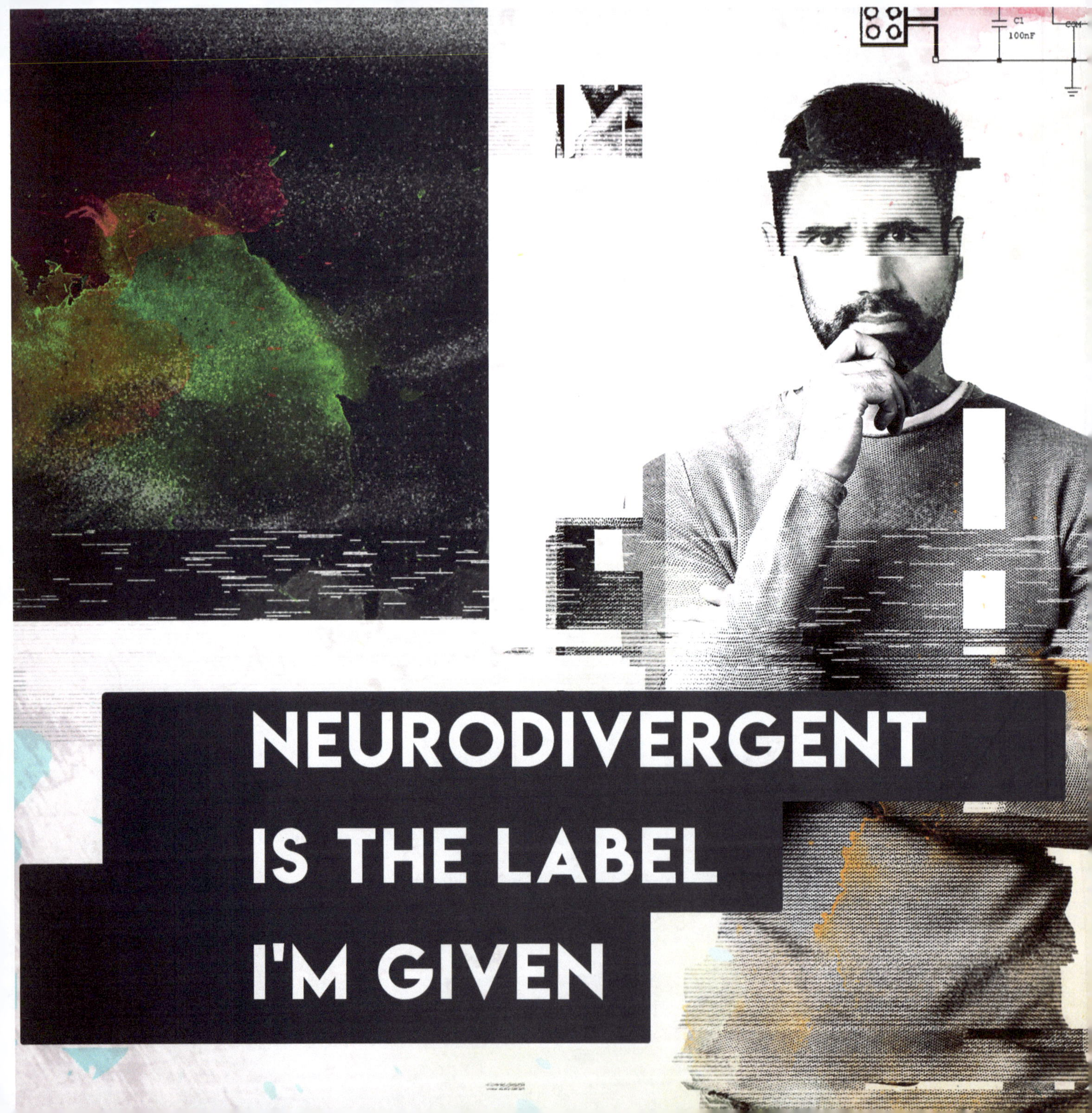
NEURODIVERGENT
IS THE LABEL
I'M GIVEN

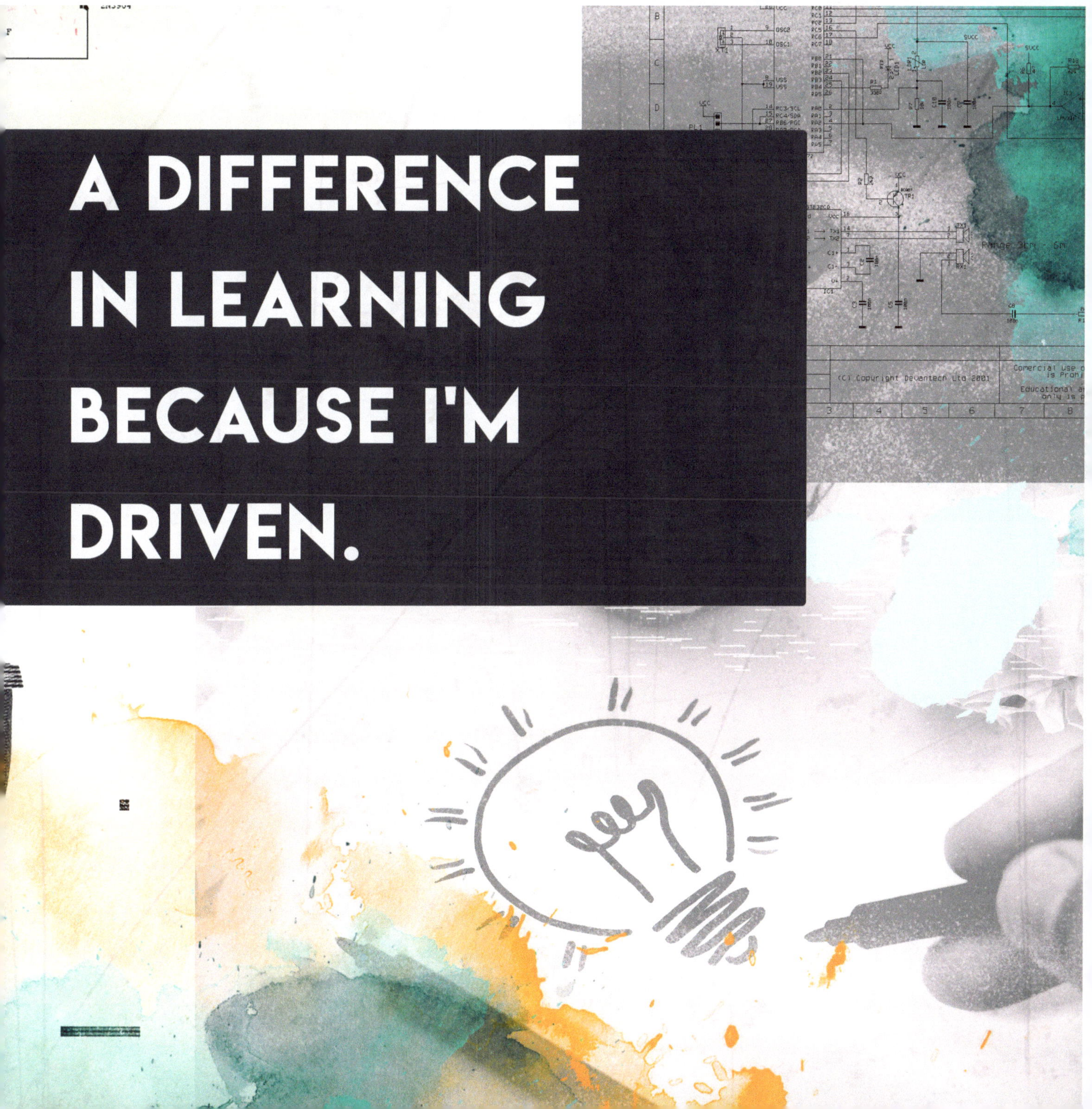
A DIFFERENCE IN LEARNING BECAUSE I'M DRIVEN.

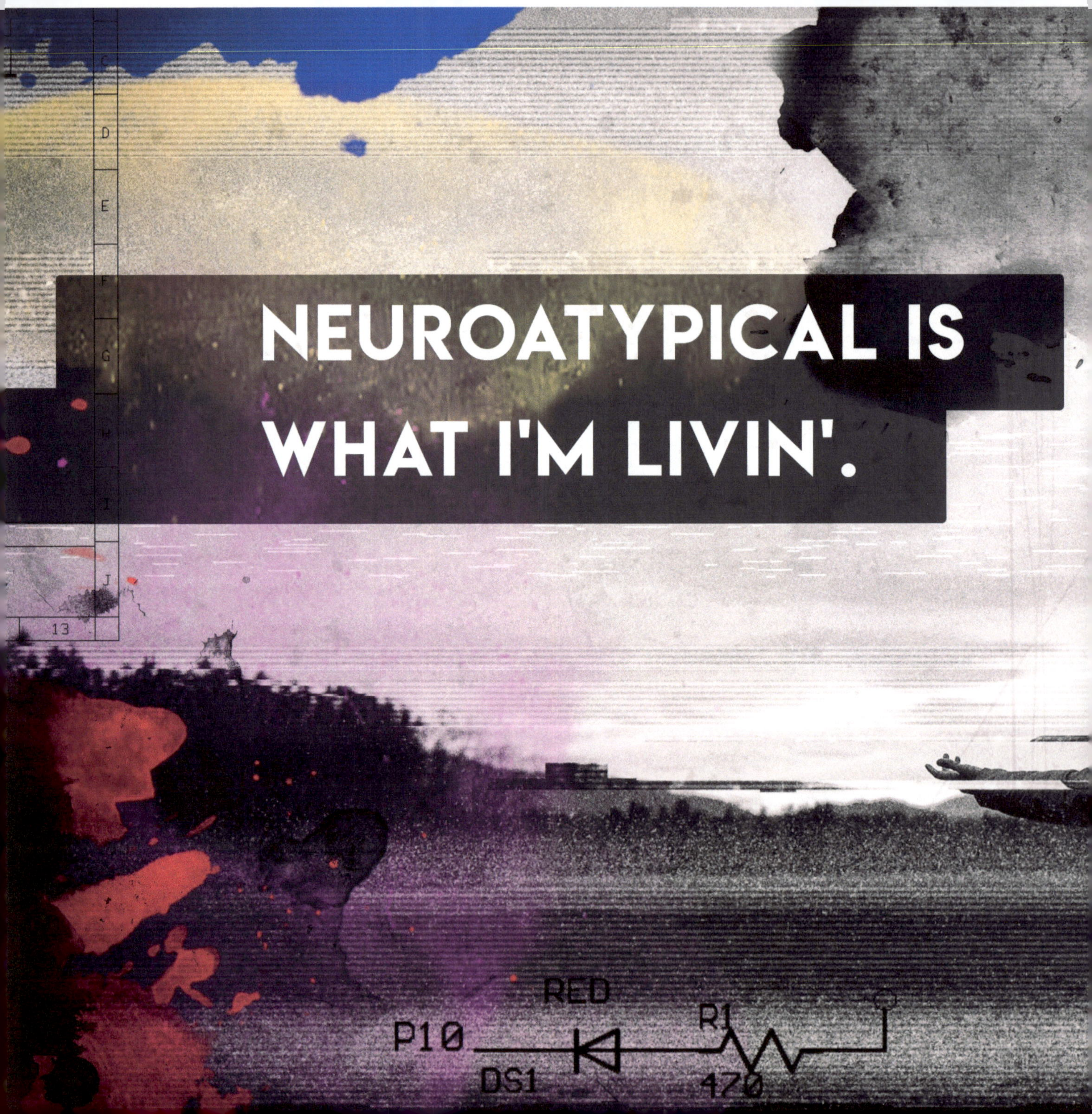

NEUROATYPICAL IS
WHAT I'M LIVIN'.

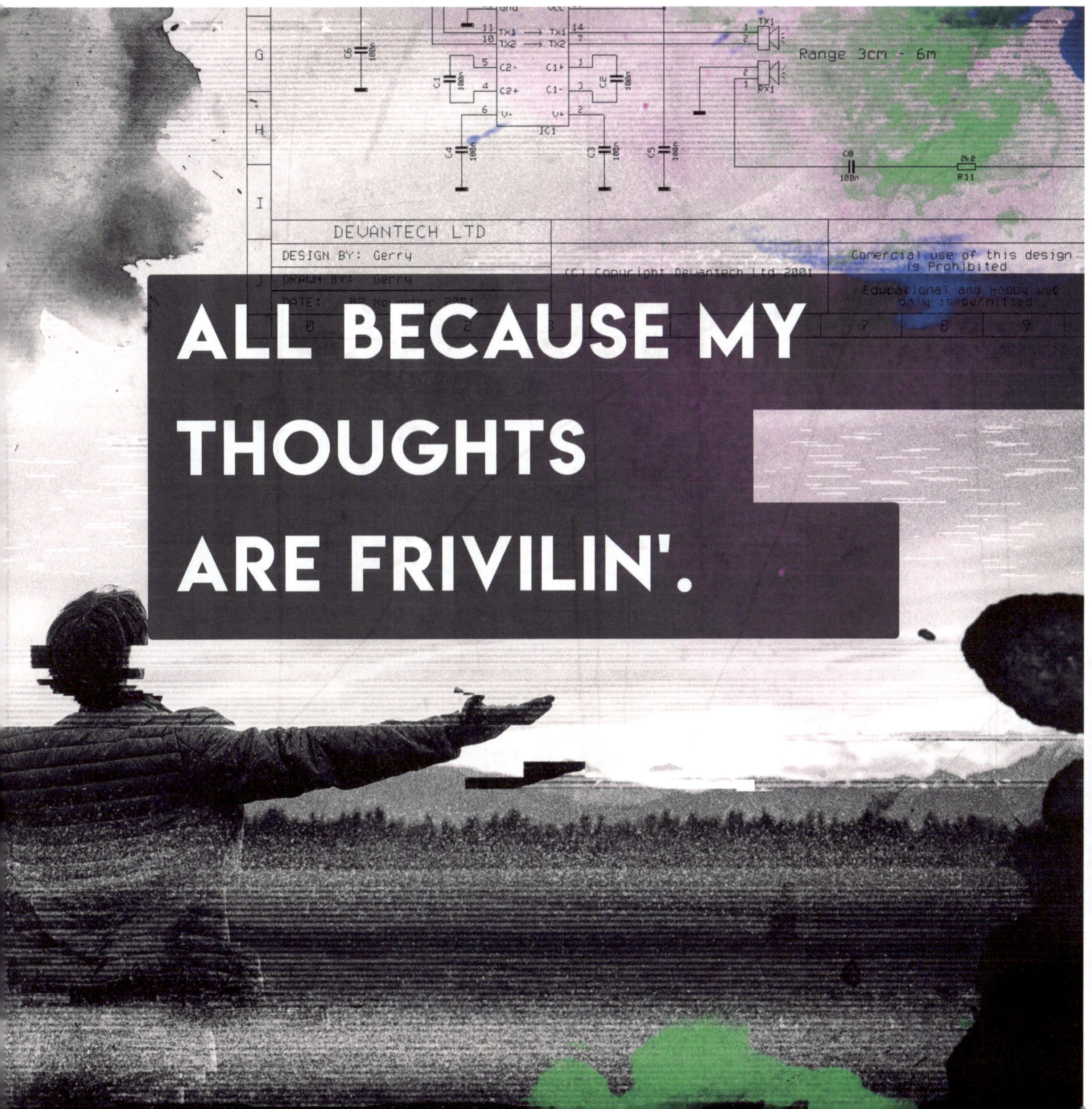

DEVANTECH LTD
DESIGN BY: Gerry
DRAWN BY: Gerry
(C) Copyright Devantech Ltd 2001
Comercial use of this design is Prohibited
Educational and Hobby use only is permitted
Range 3cm - 6m
ALL BECAUSE MY THOUGHTS ARE FRIVILIN'.

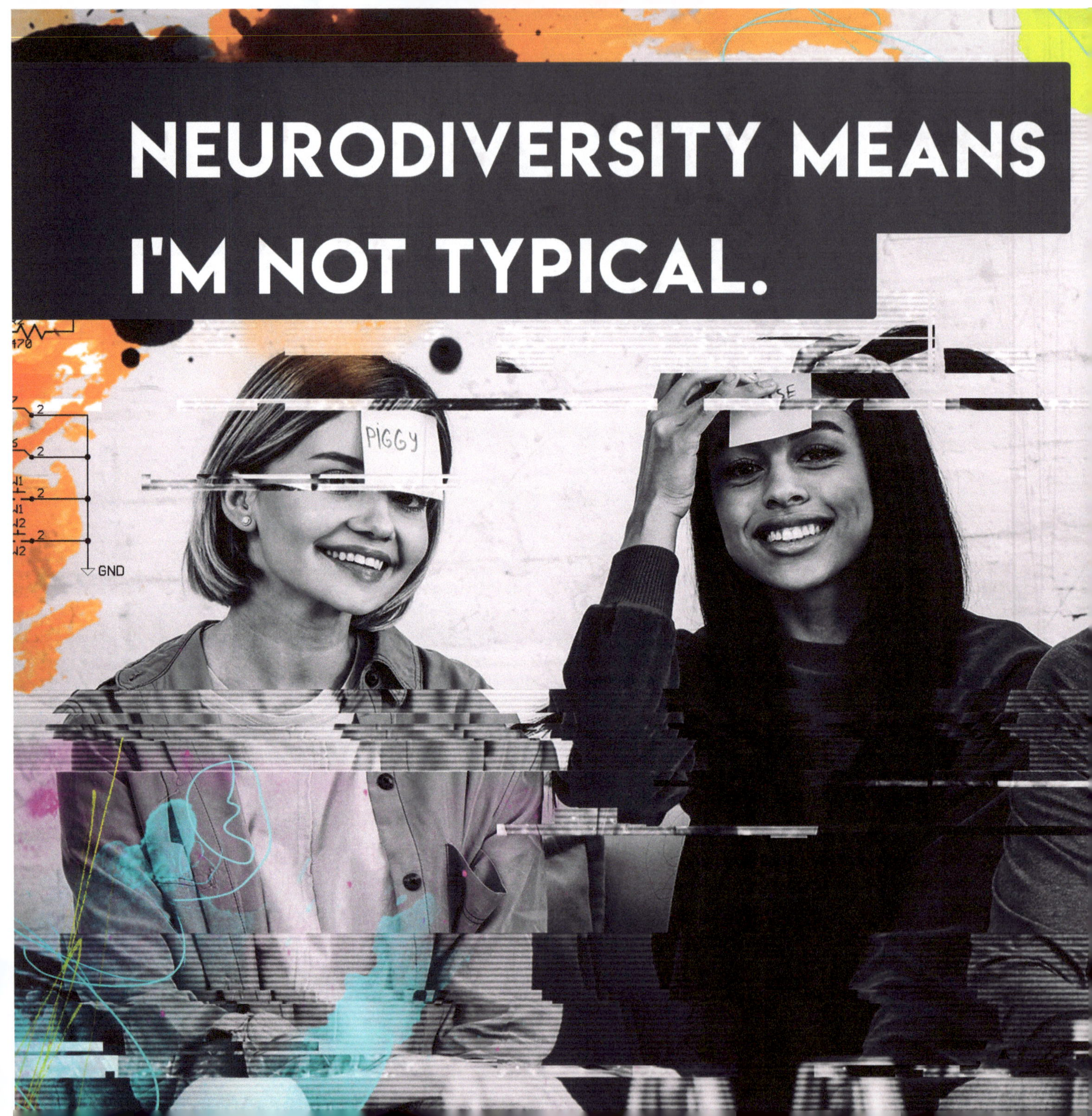
NEURODIVERSITY MEANS
I'M NOT TYPICAL.
PIGGY
GND

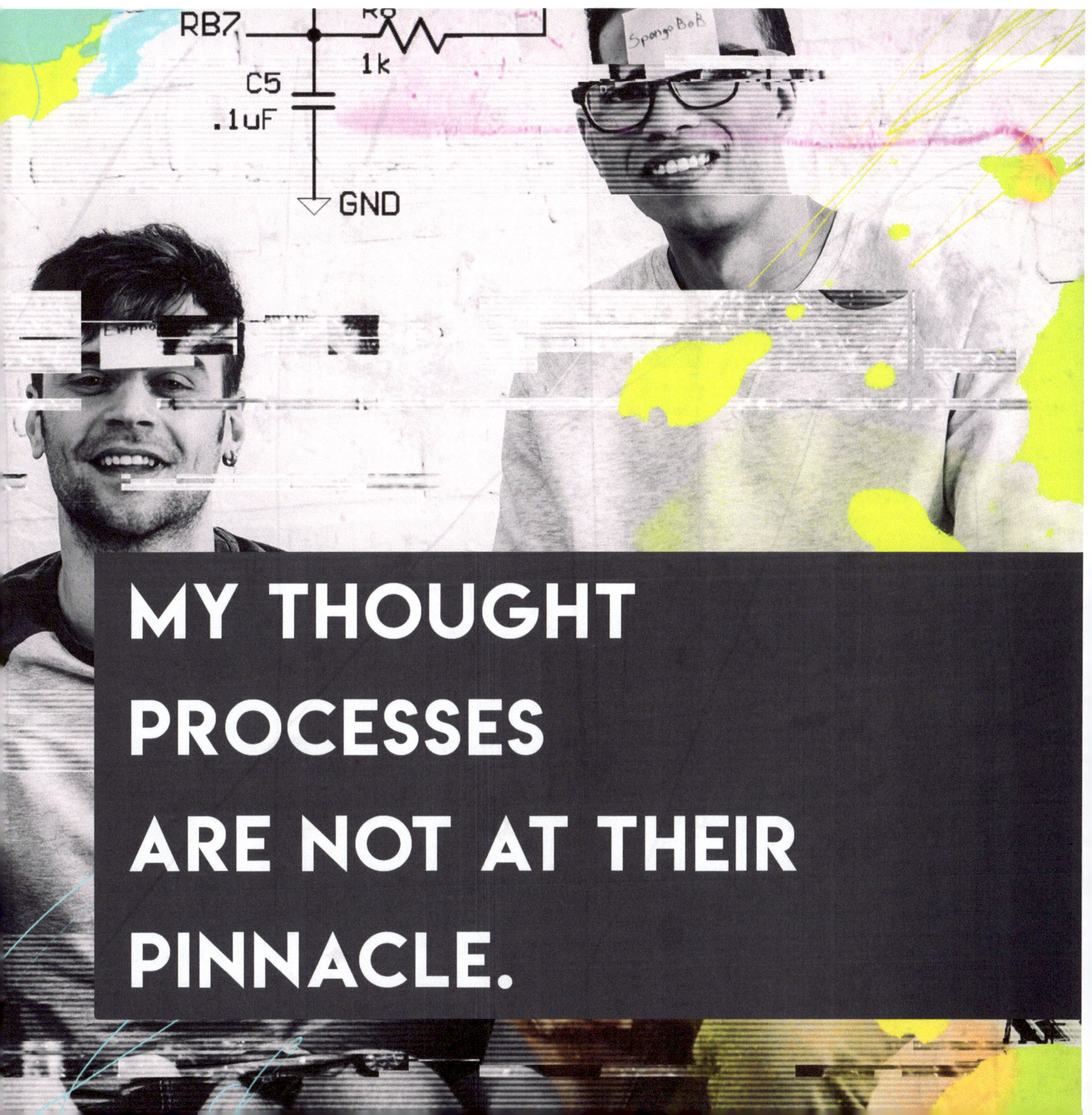

RB7
C5
.1uF
1k
GND
SpongeBoB
MY THOUGHT PROCESSES ARE NOT AT THEIR PINNACLE.

BRAIN TRAINING THEY SAY IS A MIRACLE.

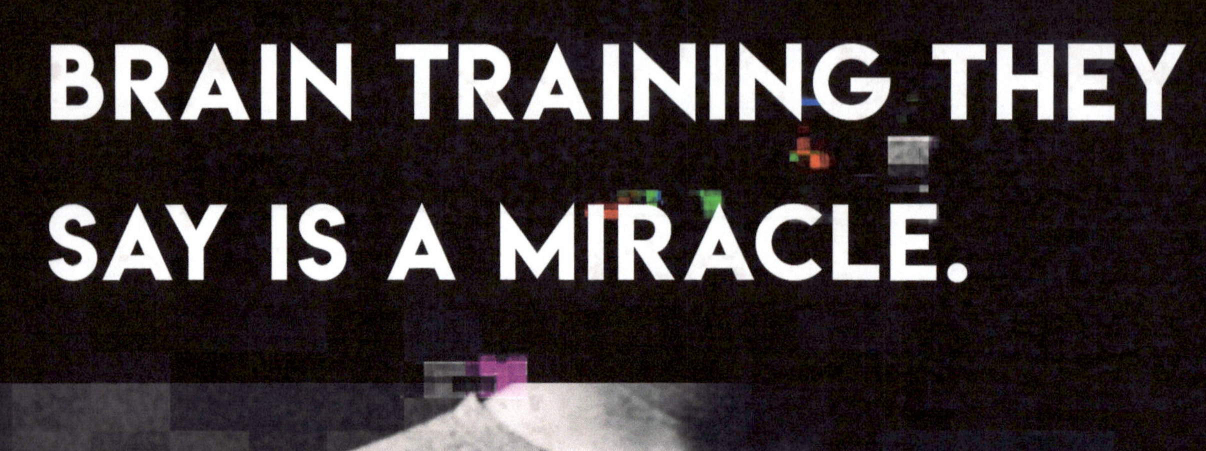

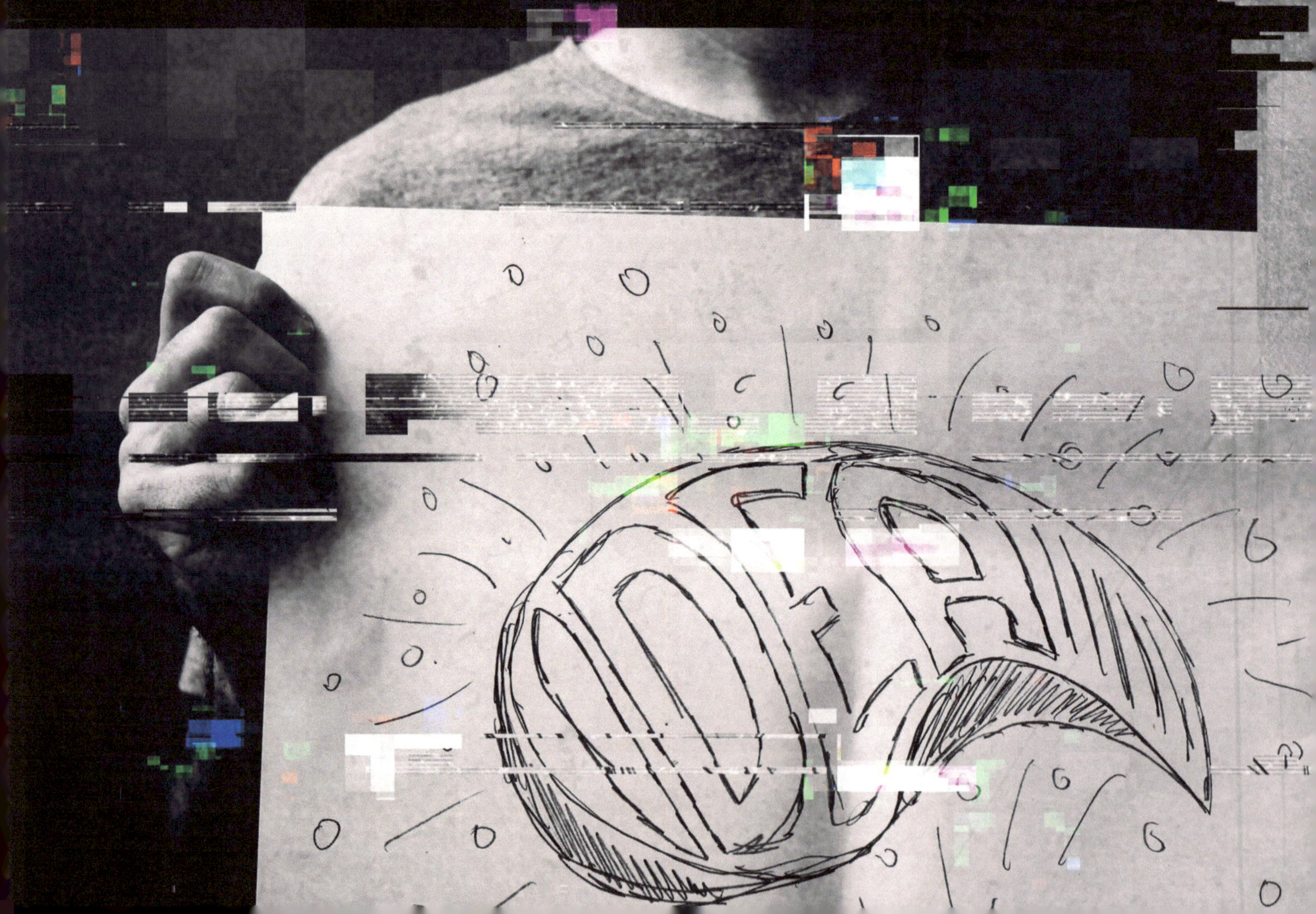

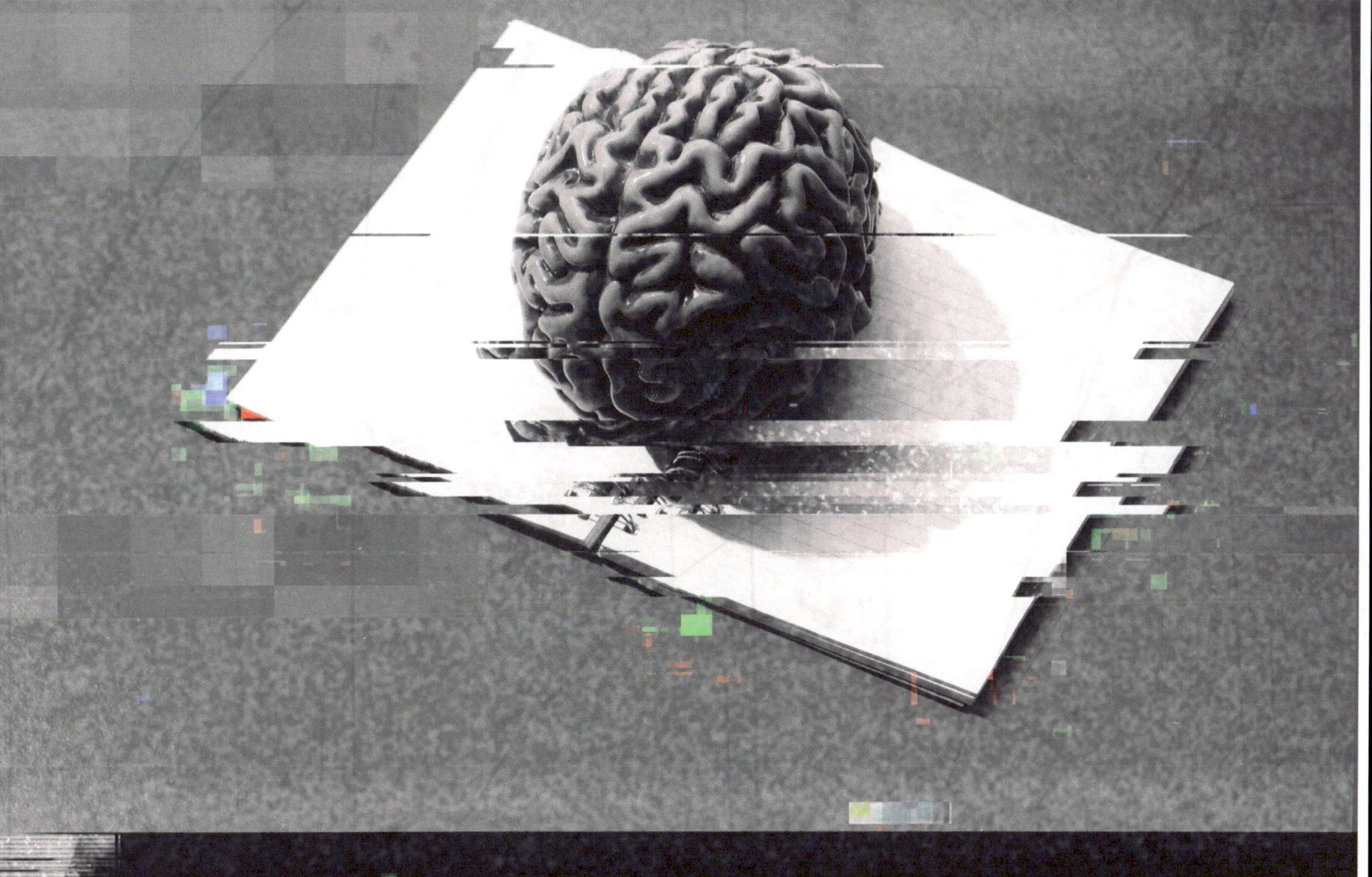

IT WILL HELP ME
BE LESS CLINICAL.

I WORK WITH A TRAINER ON THE FORMIDABLE

SO I CAN BECOME MORE ORIGINAL.

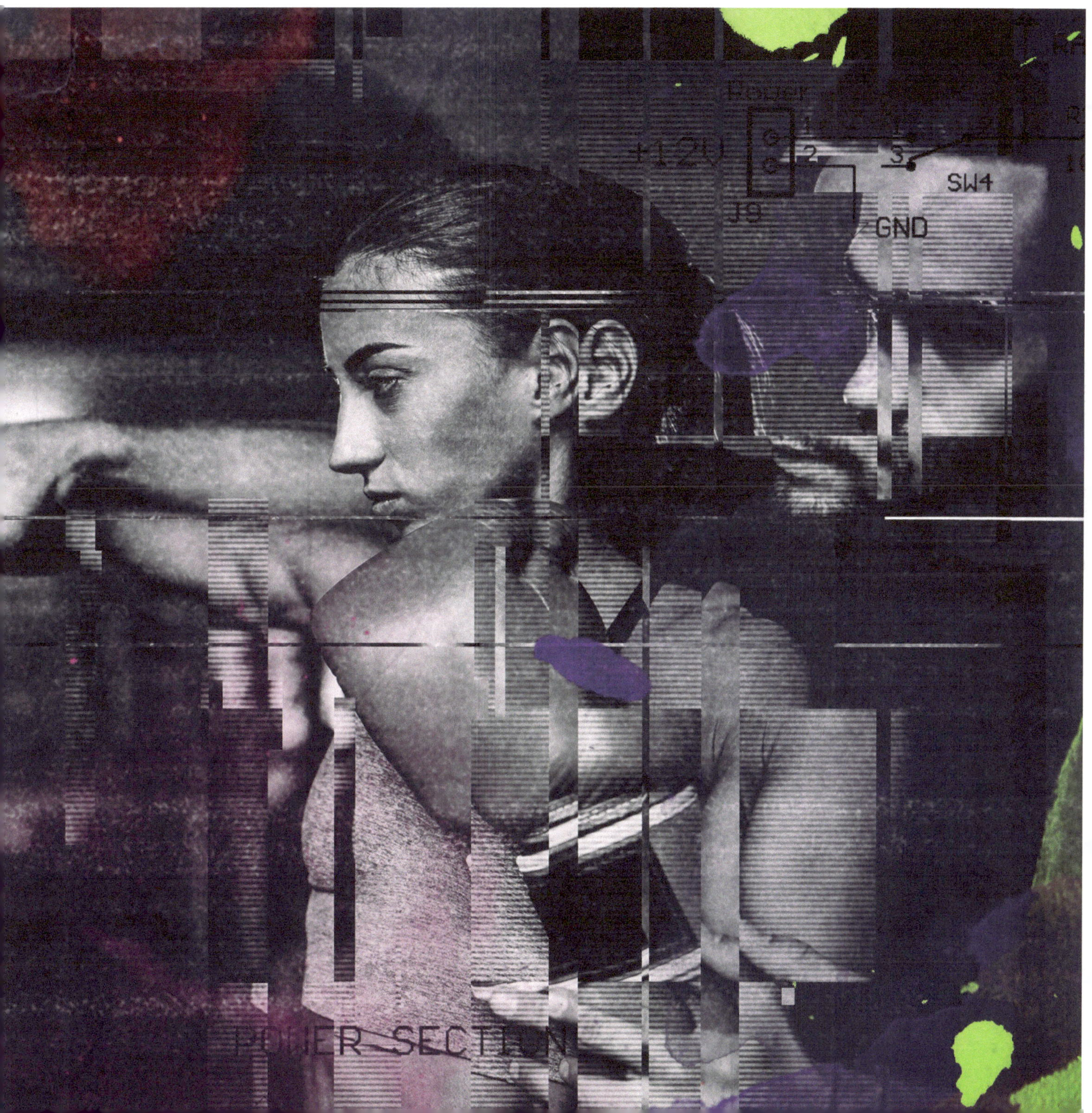
Power
+12V
J9
GND
SW4
POWER SECTION

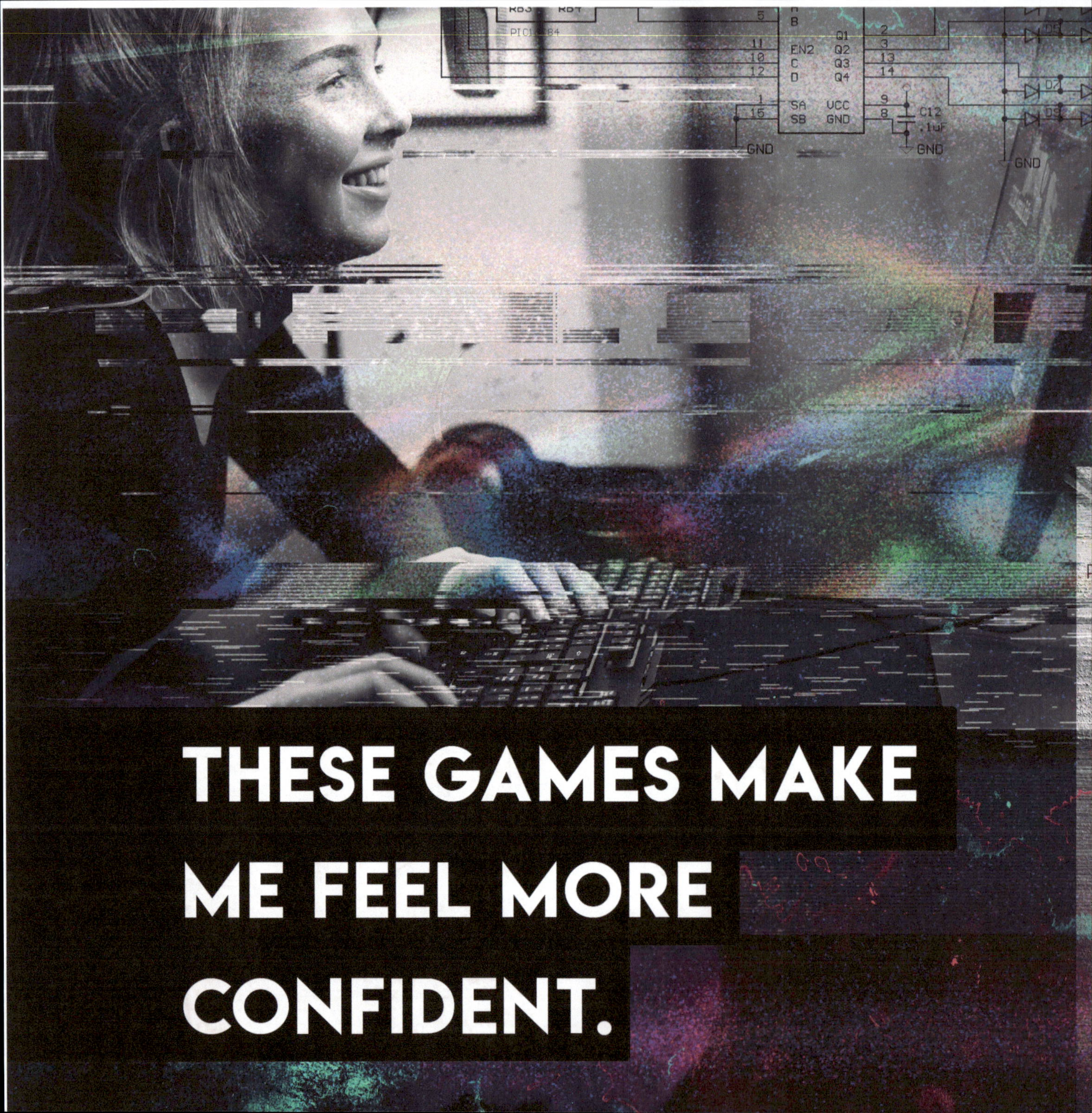
THESE GAMES MAKE ME FEEL MORE CONFIDENT.

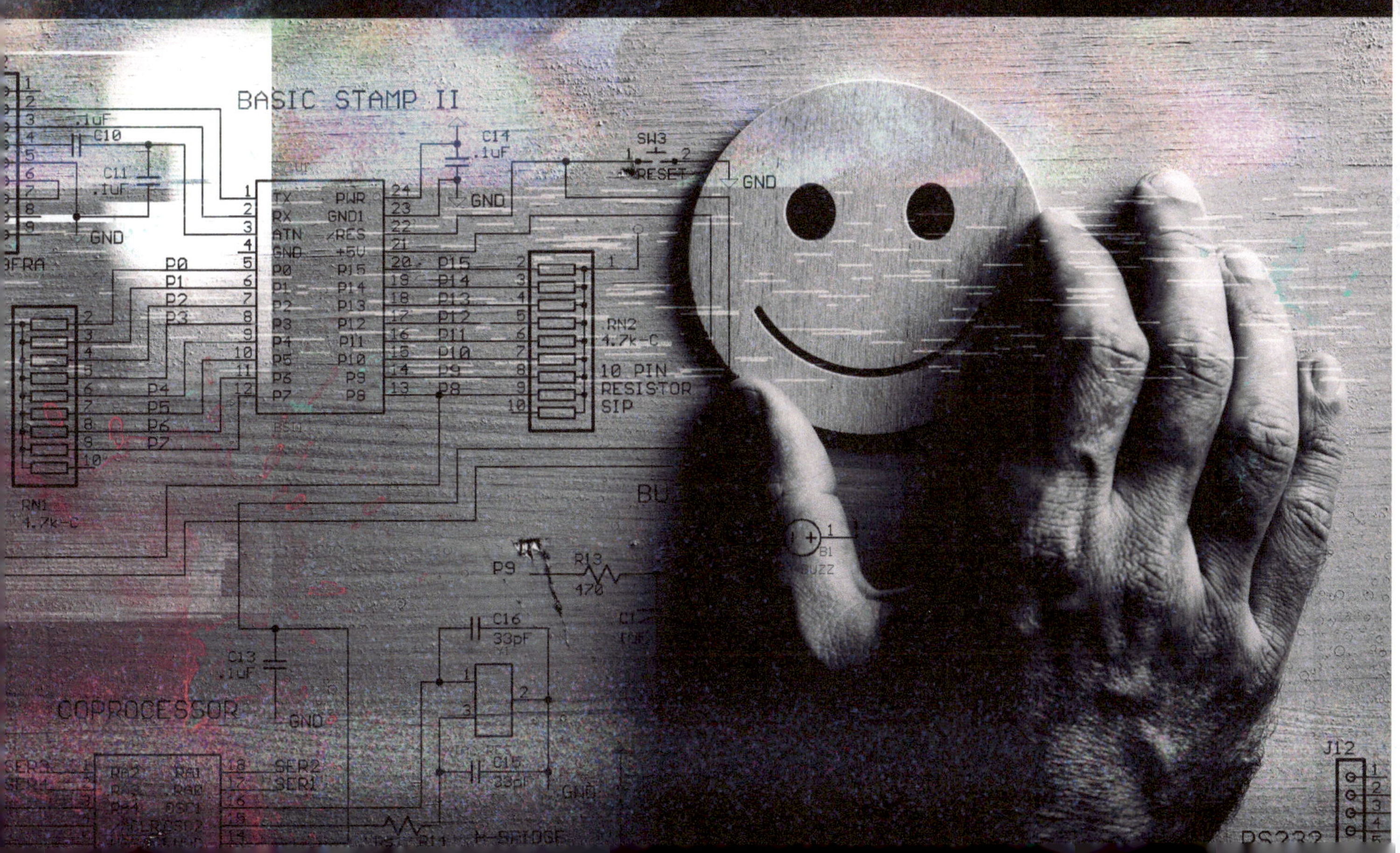
I RELEARN THE CODES OF VOWELS AND CONSONANTS.
MOTOR
.1uF
C7
M2
POWERFUL
OUTPUT
BASIC STAMP II
C10
.1uF
C11
.1uF
GND
C14
.1uF
GND
SW3
RESET
GND
3FRA
TX   PWR   24
RX   GND1   23
ATN   /RES   22
GND   +5U   21
P0   P15   20   P15
P1   P14   19   P14
P2   P13   18   P13
P3   P12   17   P12
P4   P11   16   P11
P5   P10   15   P10
P6   P9   14   P9
P7   P8   13   P8
RN2
4.7k-C
10 PIN
RESISTOR
SIP
RN1
4.7k-C
BU
P9   R13
470
C16
33pF
C13
.1uF
COPROCESSOR
GND
C15
33pF
GND
B1
BUZZ
SER2
SER1
J12
RS232

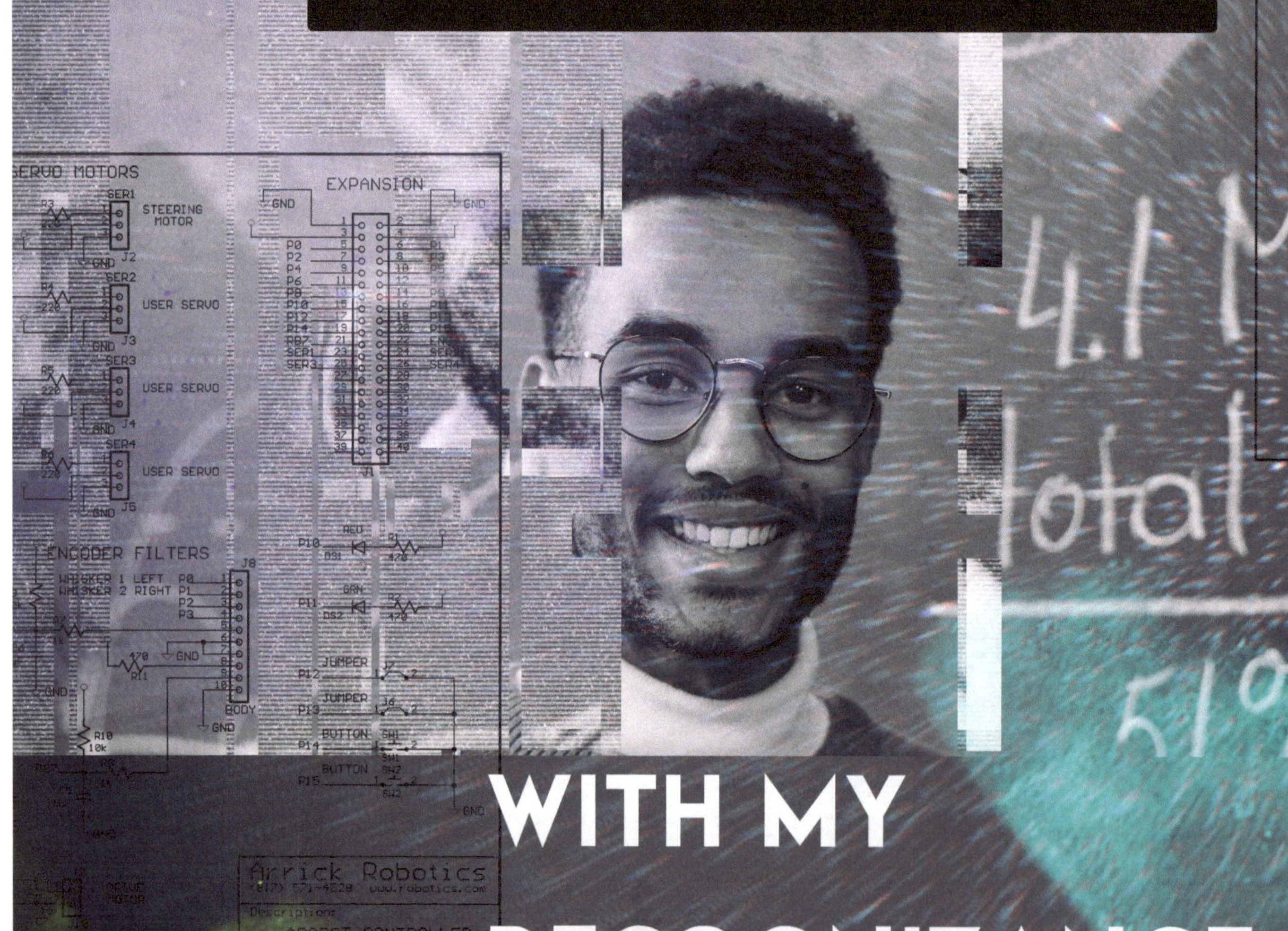
MY BRAIN
COACH HELPS ME
WITH MY
RECOGNIZANCE

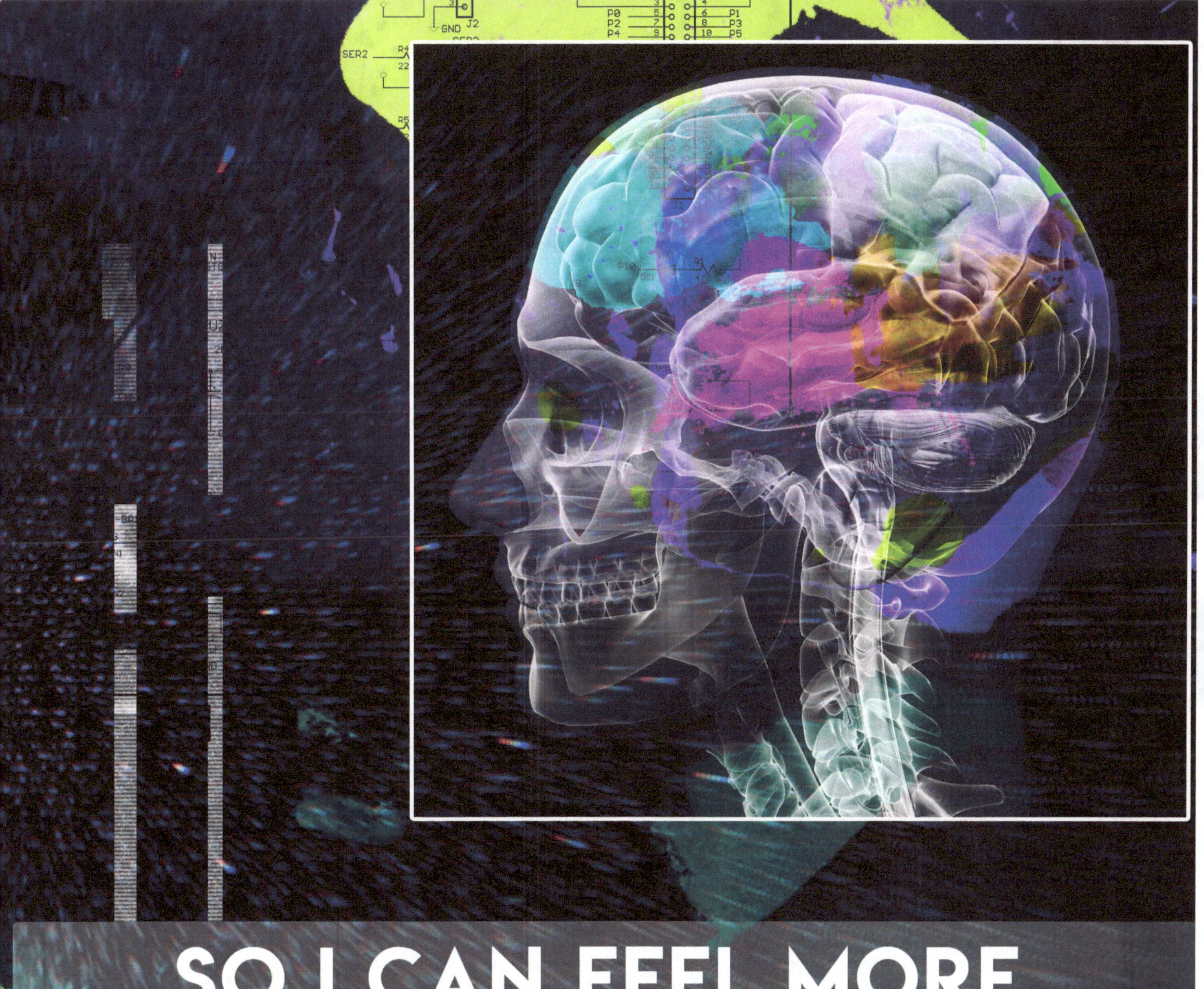

SO I CAN FEEL MORE PREPONDERANT.

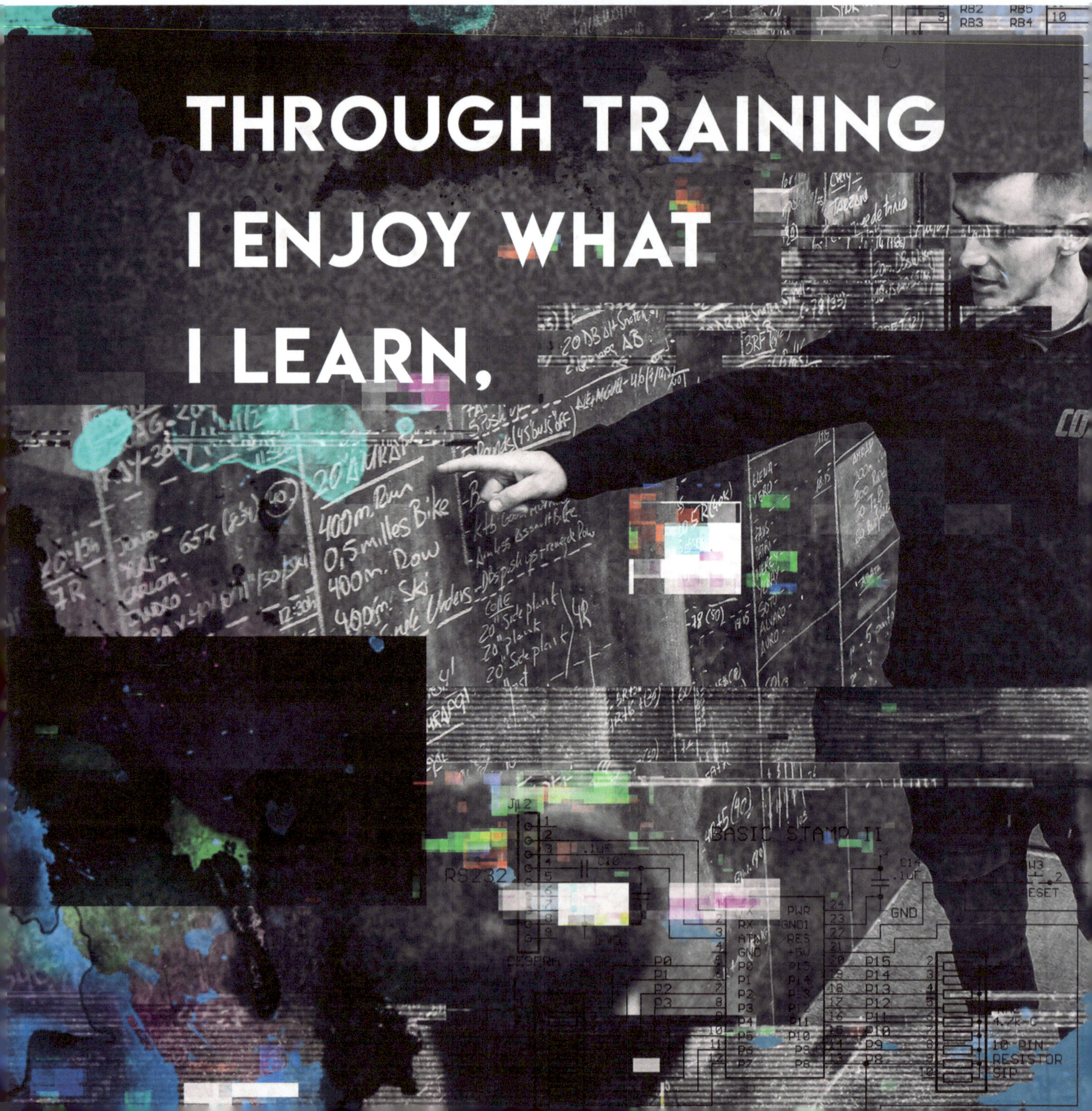

THROUGH TRAINING
I ENJOY WHAT
I LEARN,

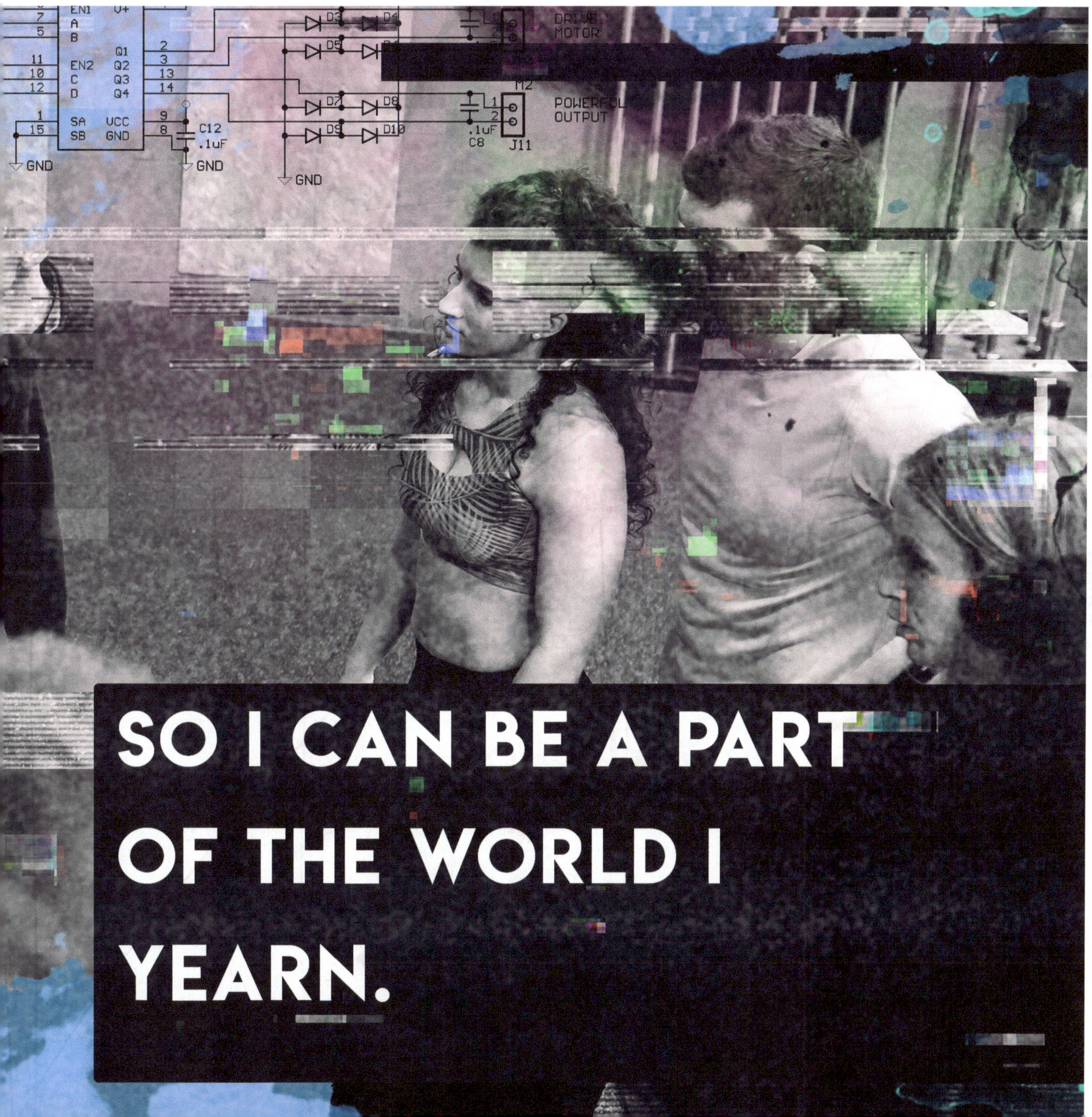

EN1
A
B
Q1
EN2
Q2
Q3
D
Q4
SA   VCC
SB   GND
GND
C12
.1uF
GND
DRIVE
MOTOR
POWERFUL
OUTPUT
.1uF
C8
J11
GND
SO I CAN BE A PART
OF THE WORLD I
YEARN.

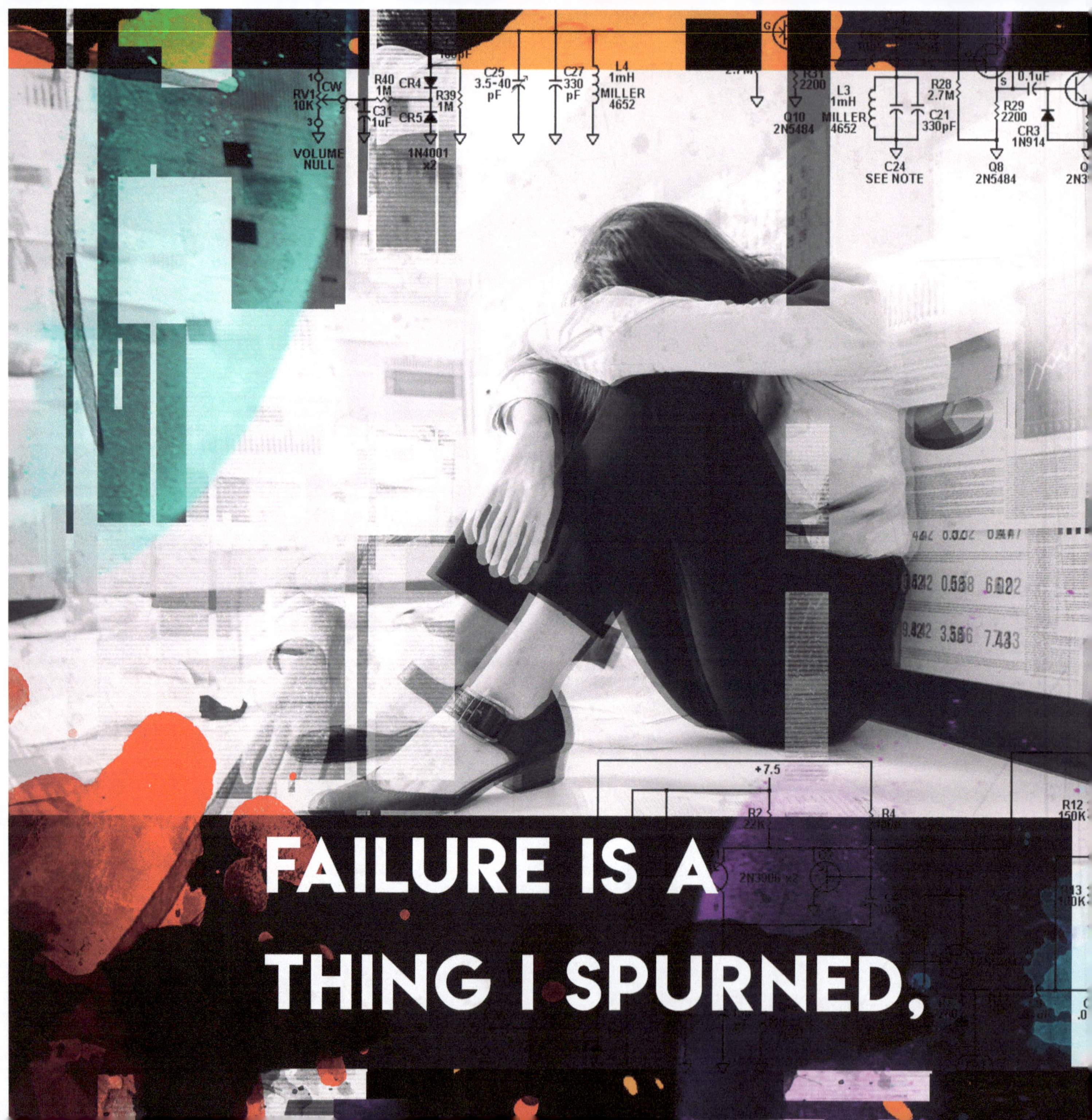

FAILURE IS A
THING I SPURNED,

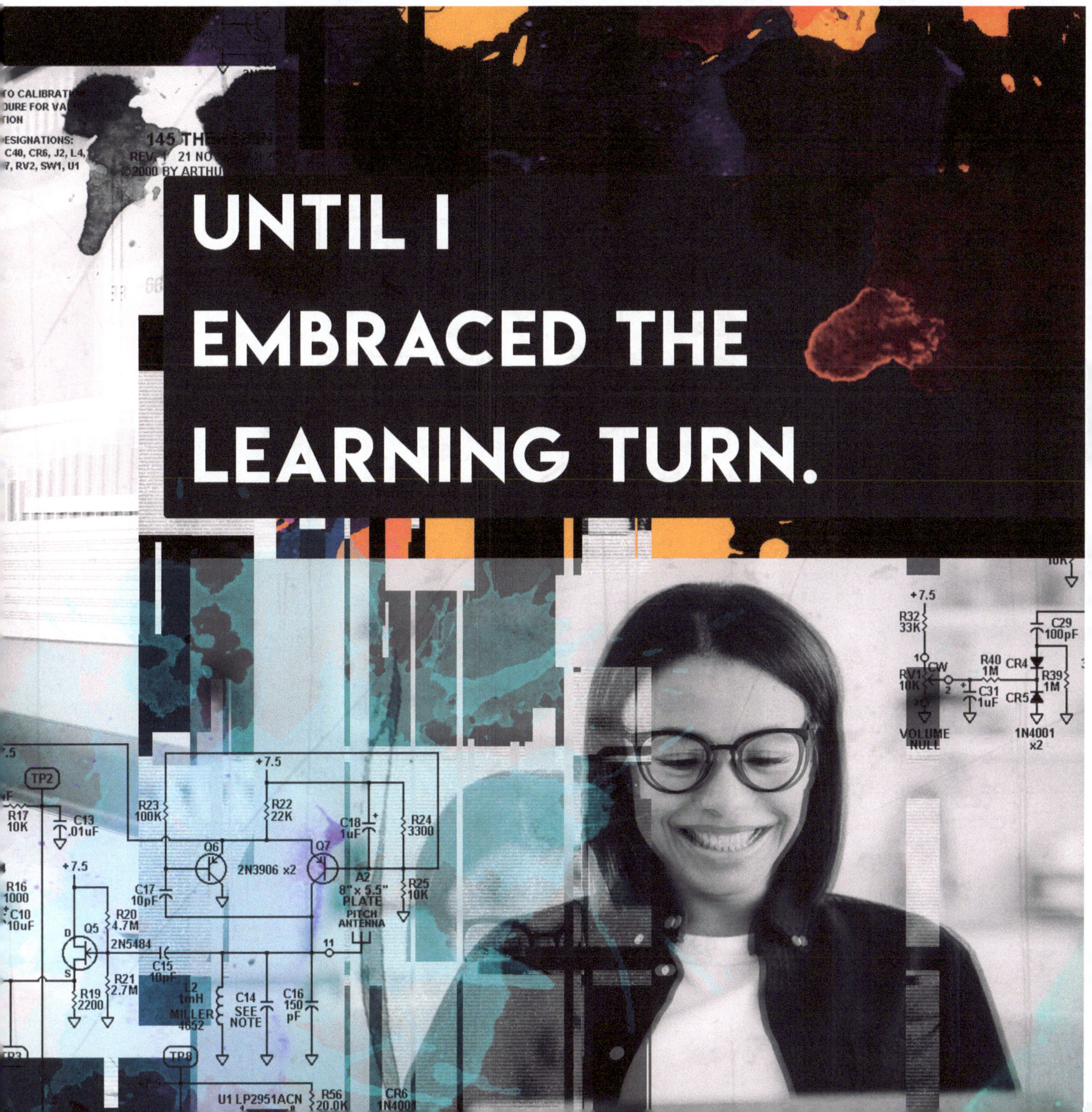

UNTIL I EMBRACED THE LEARNING TURN.

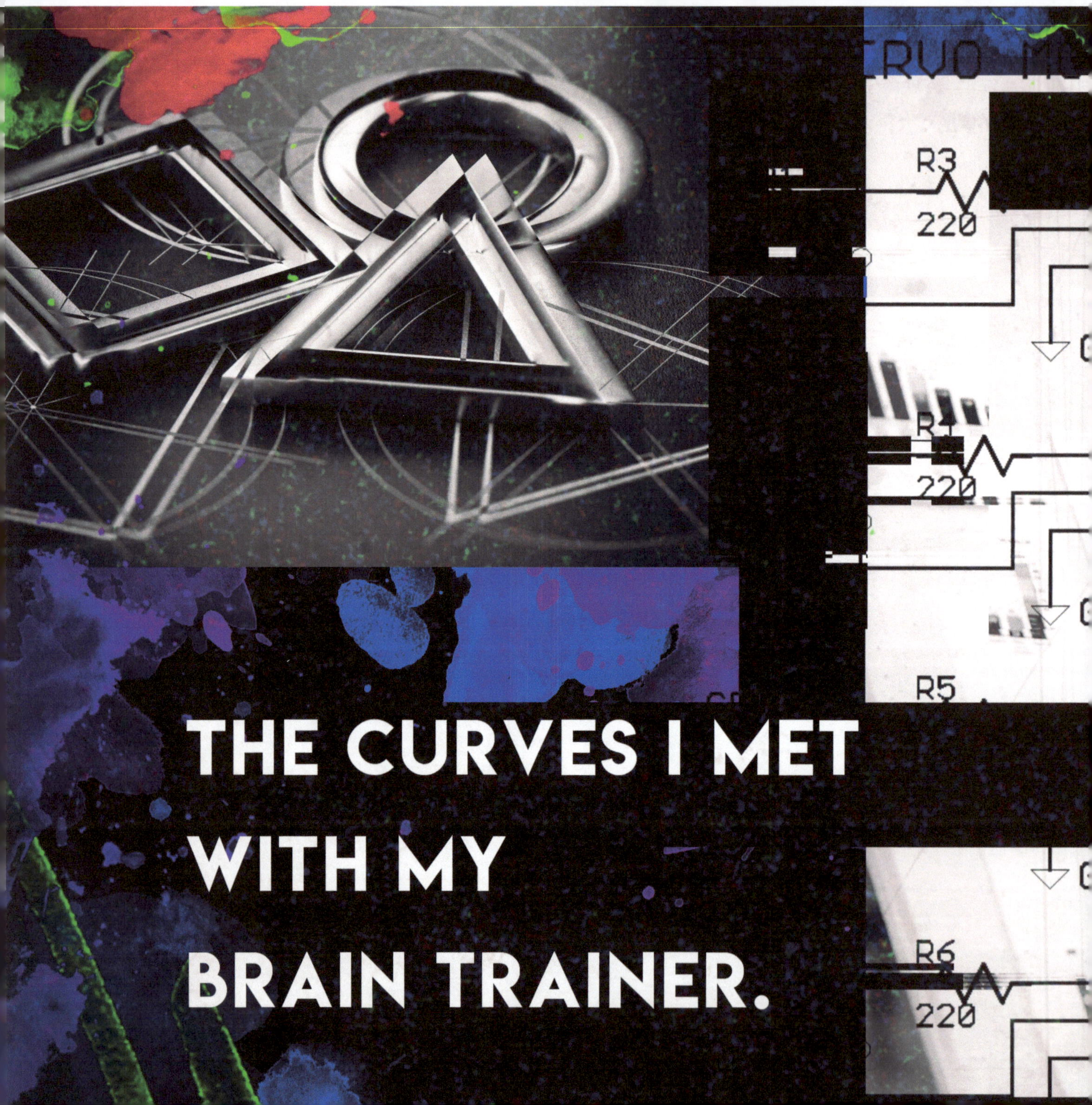
THE CURVES I MET
WITH MY
BRAIN TRAINER.
R3
220
R1
220
R5
R6
220

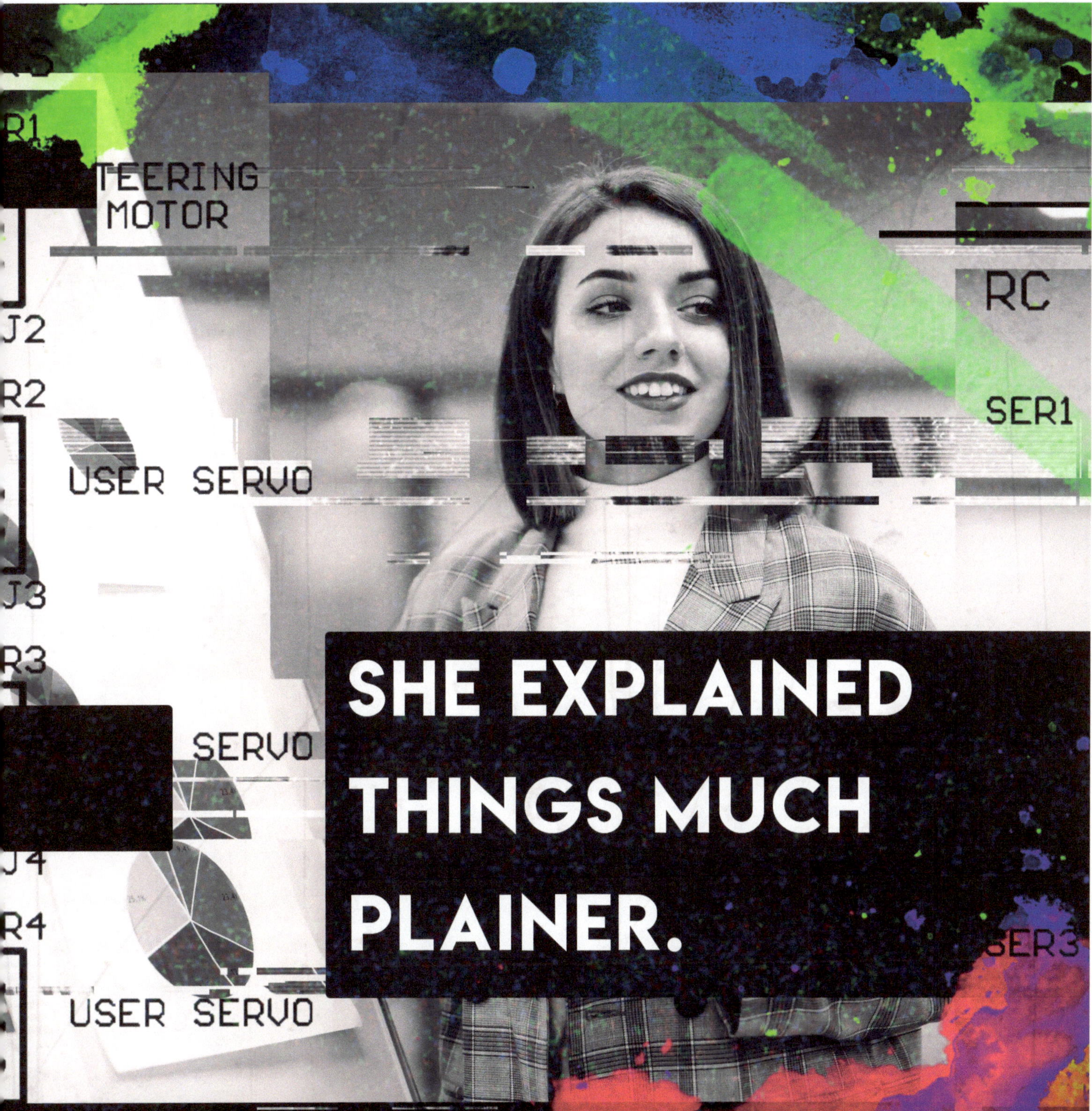
R1
TEERING MOTOR
J2
R2
USER SERVO
J3
R3
SERVO
J4
R4
USER SERVO
RC
SER1
SER3
SHE EXPLAINED THINGS MUCH PLAINER.

NOW I KNOW THAT AS A DIVERGENT THINKER,

I HAVE A GIFT THAT ISN'T WEAKER.

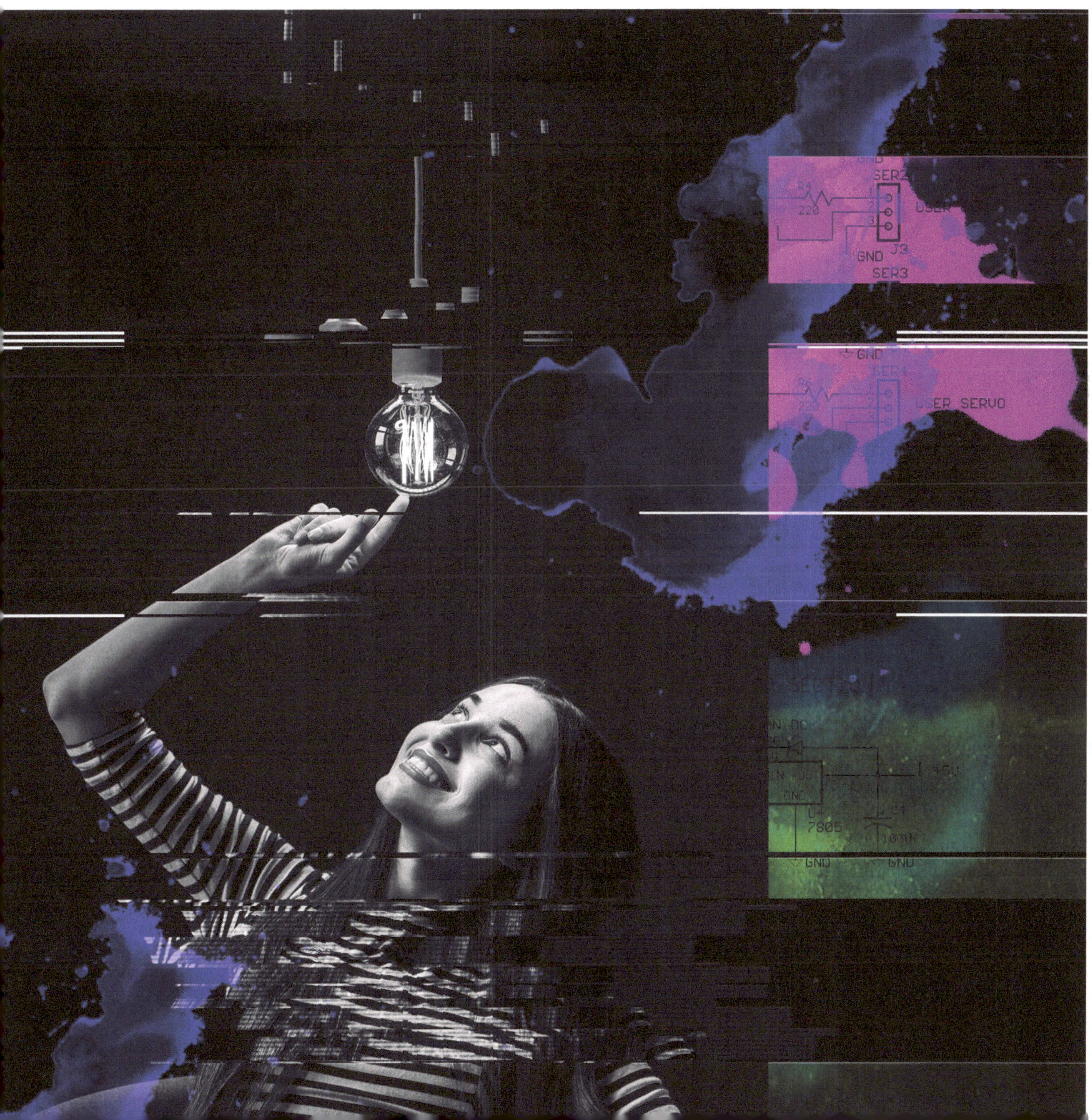

GND
SER2
USER
220
GND
J3
SER3
GND
SER4
220
USER SERVO
IN DC
7805
GND
GND
GND

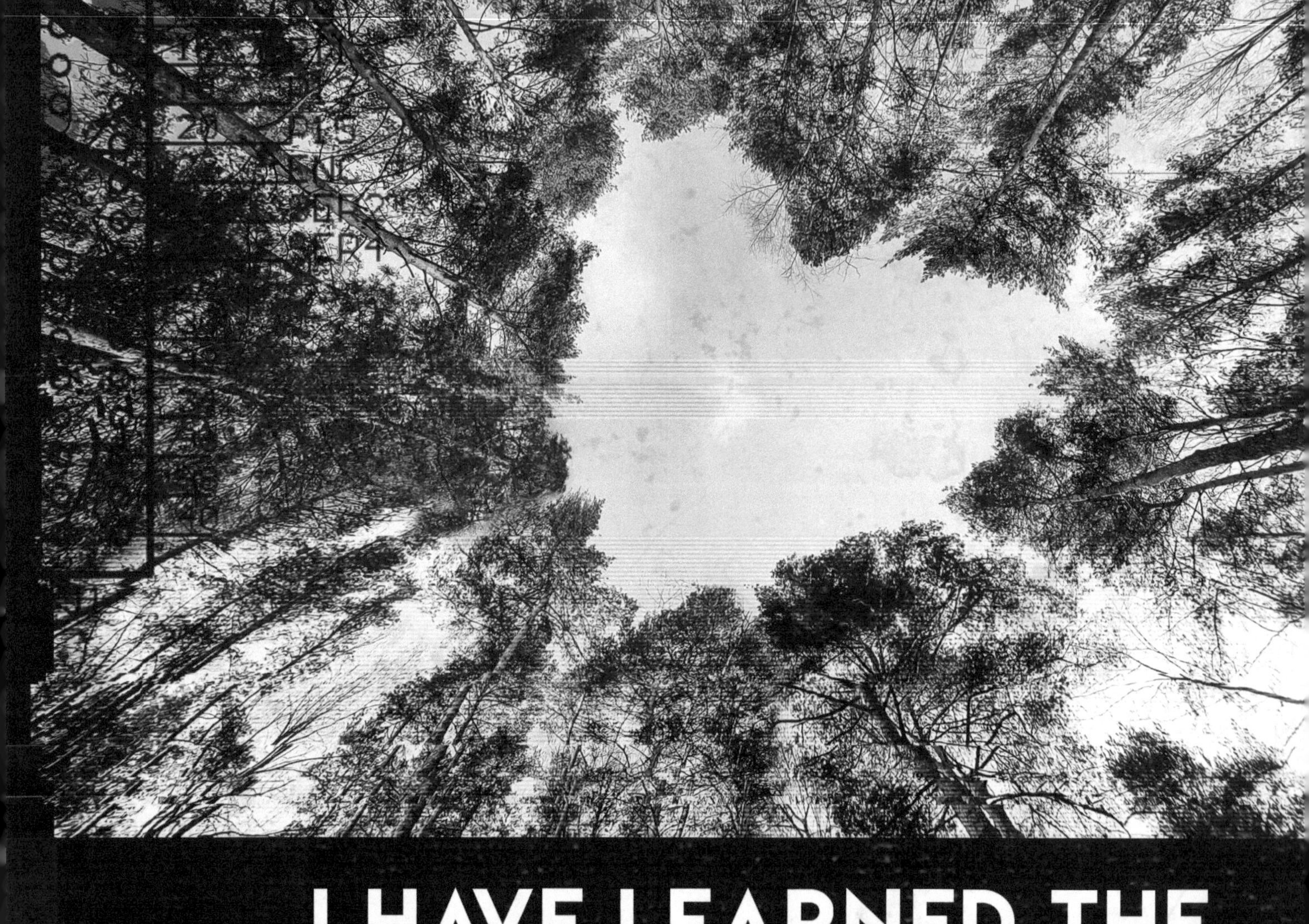

I HAVE LEARNED THE
WAY TO LEARNING

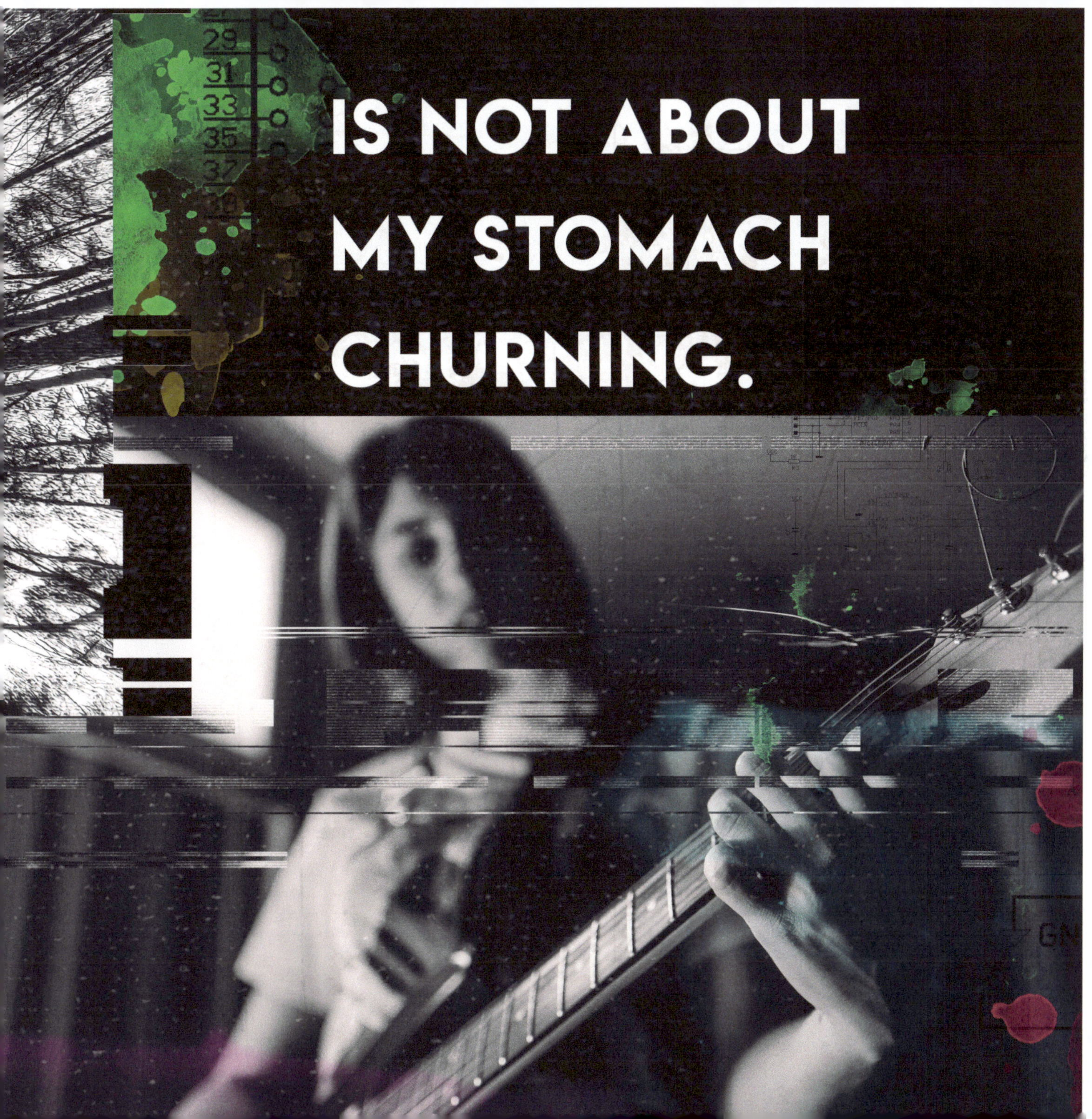
IS NOT ABOUT MY STOMACH CHURNING.

MY ANXIETY IS A THING OF TURNING

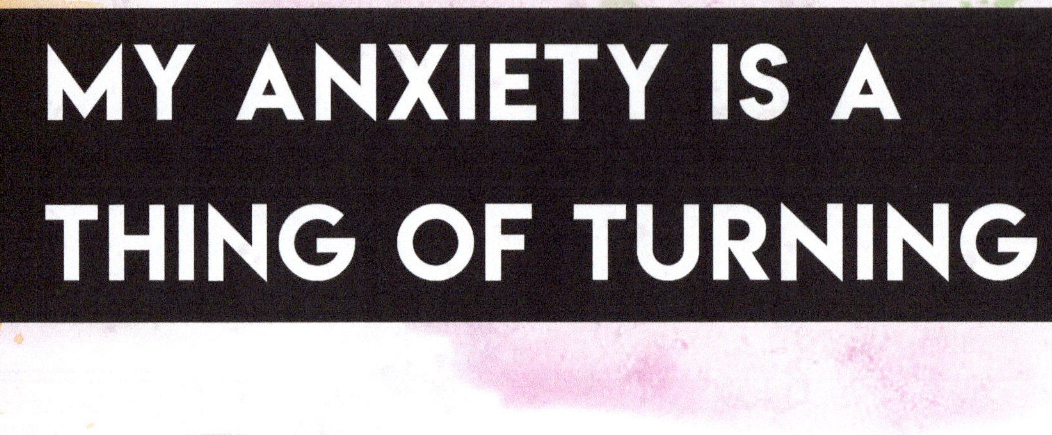

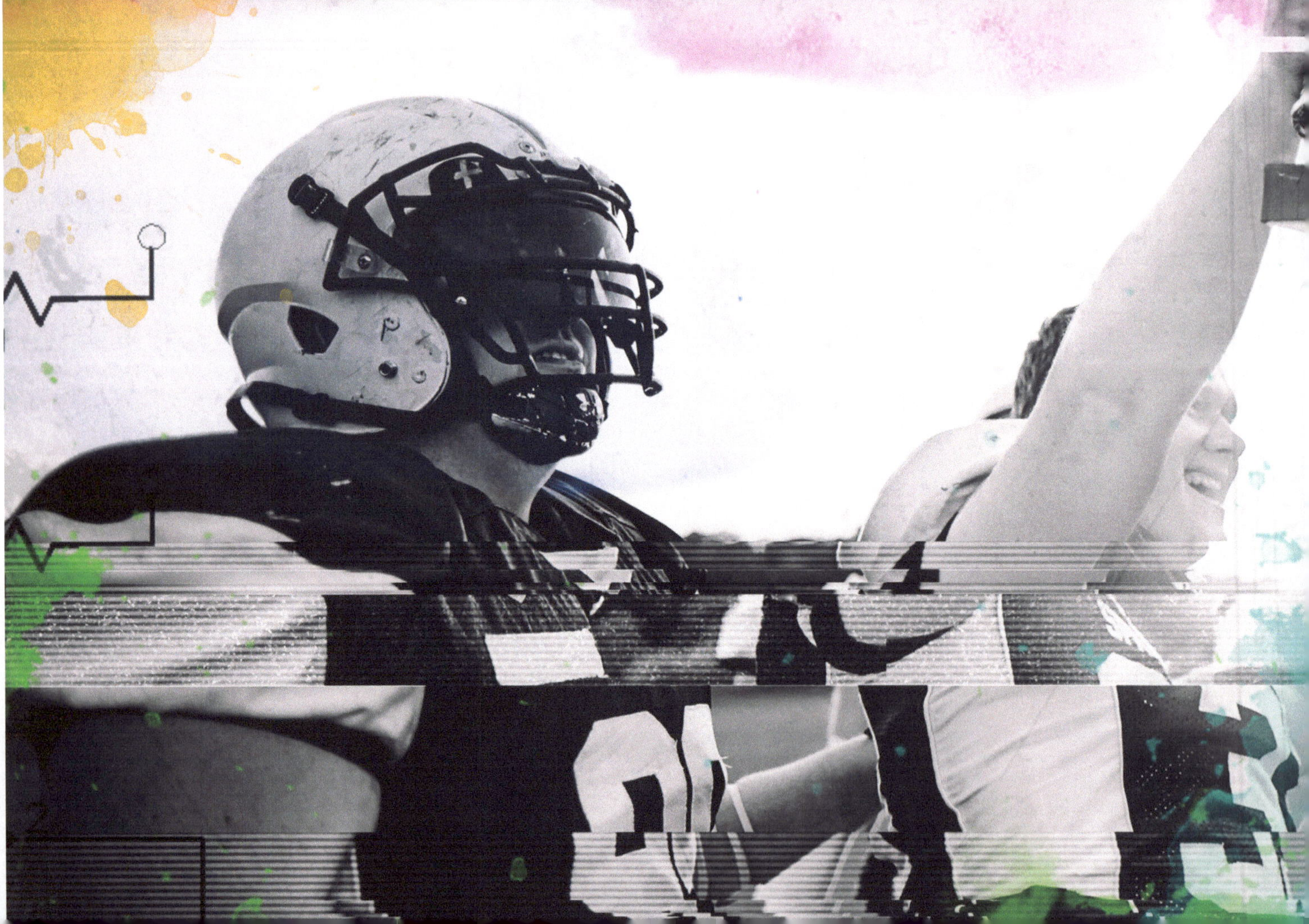

THE HARD THINGS INTO PLAYFUL EARNINGS.

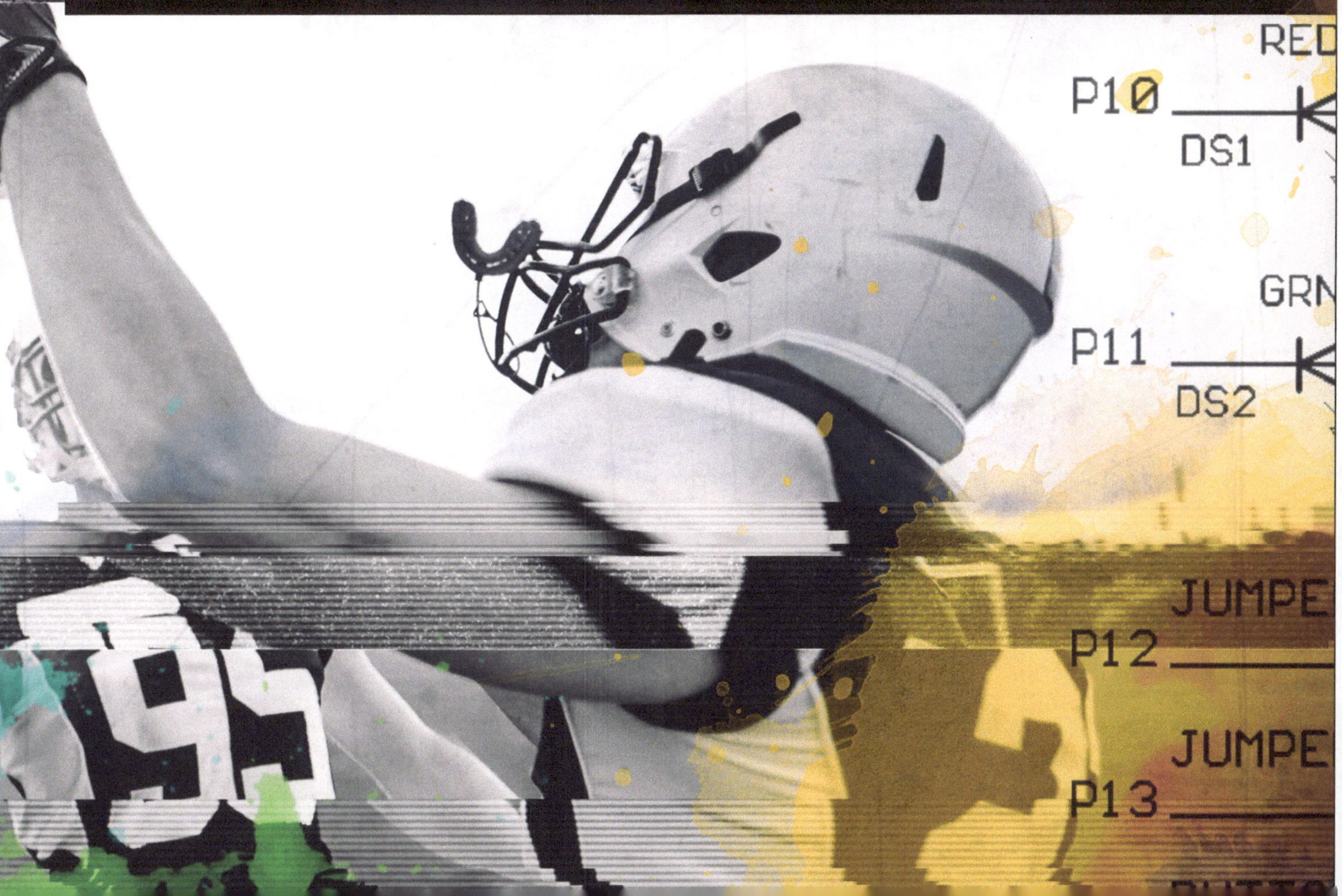

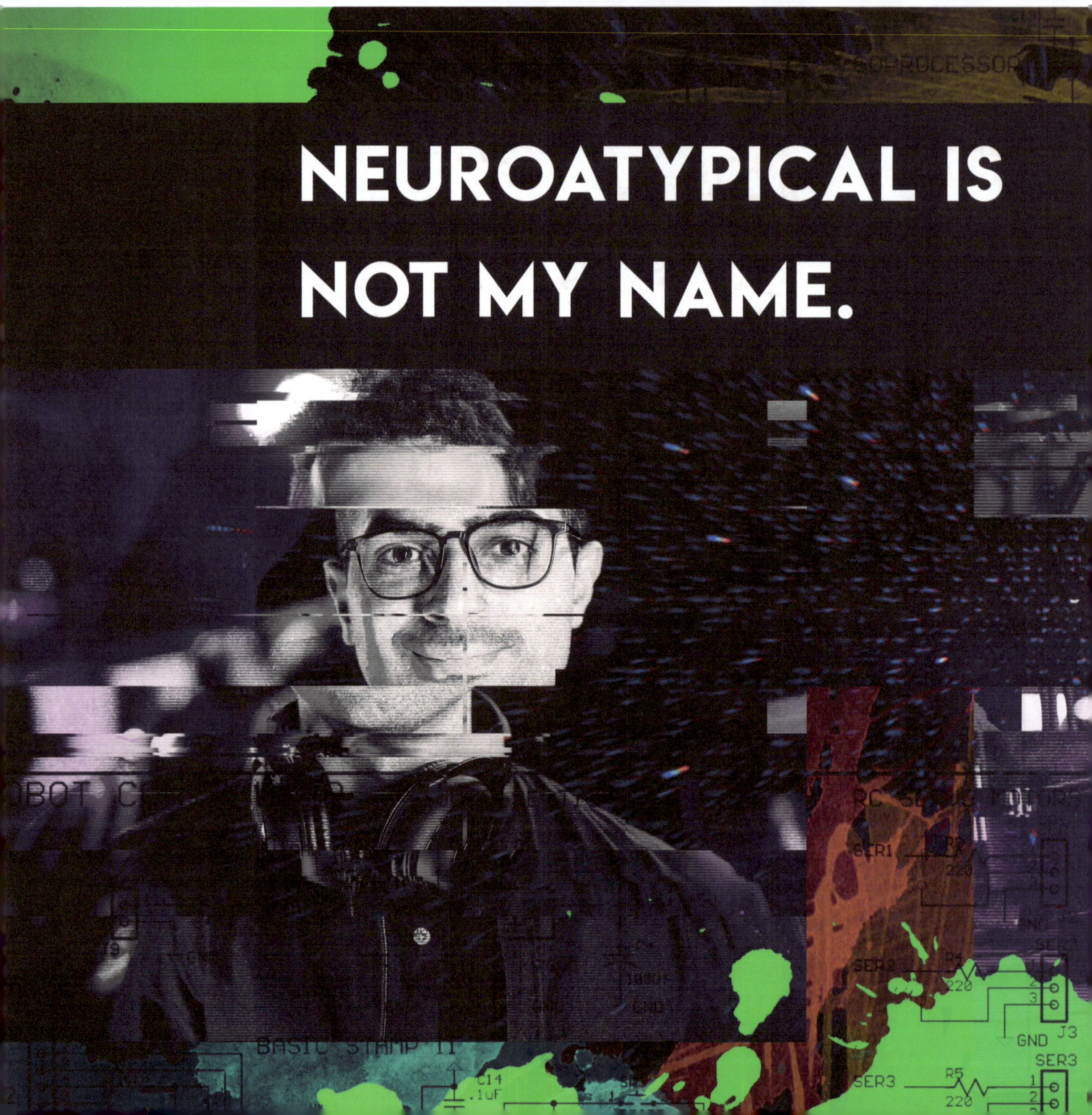
NEUROATYPICAL IS
NOT MY NAME.

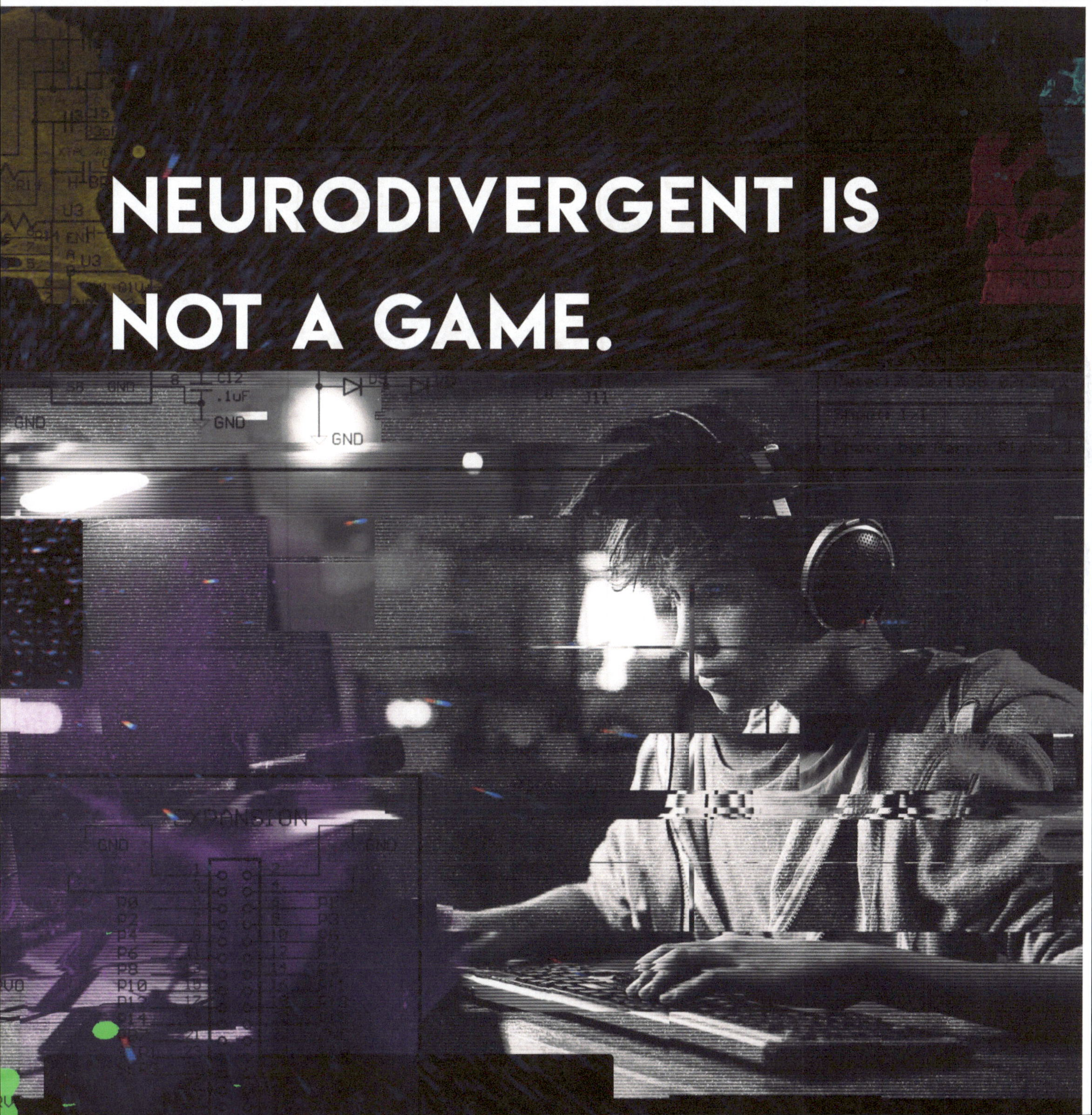

NEURODIVERGENT IS
NOT A GAME.

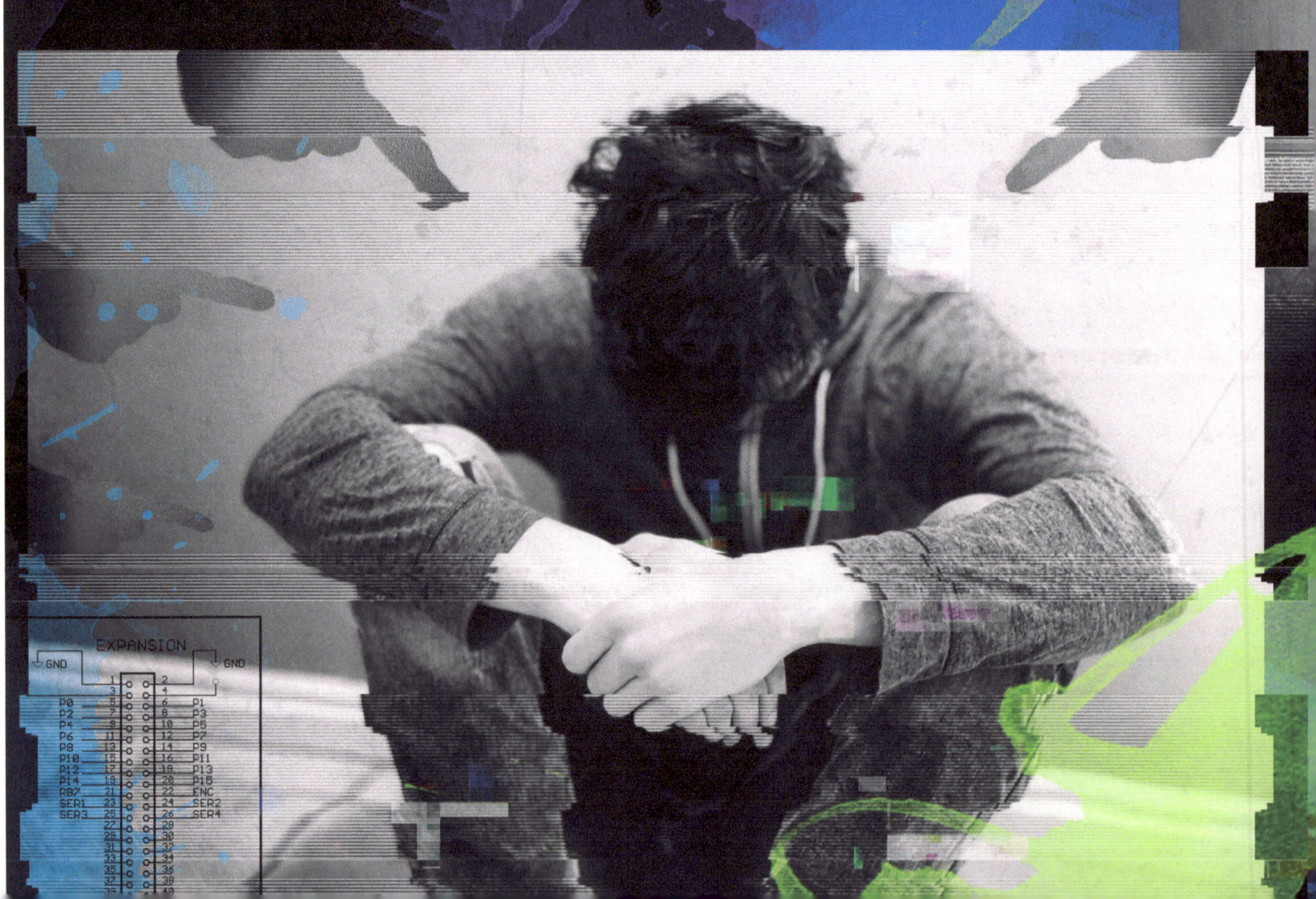
NEUROVARIANCE
IS NOT BLAME.

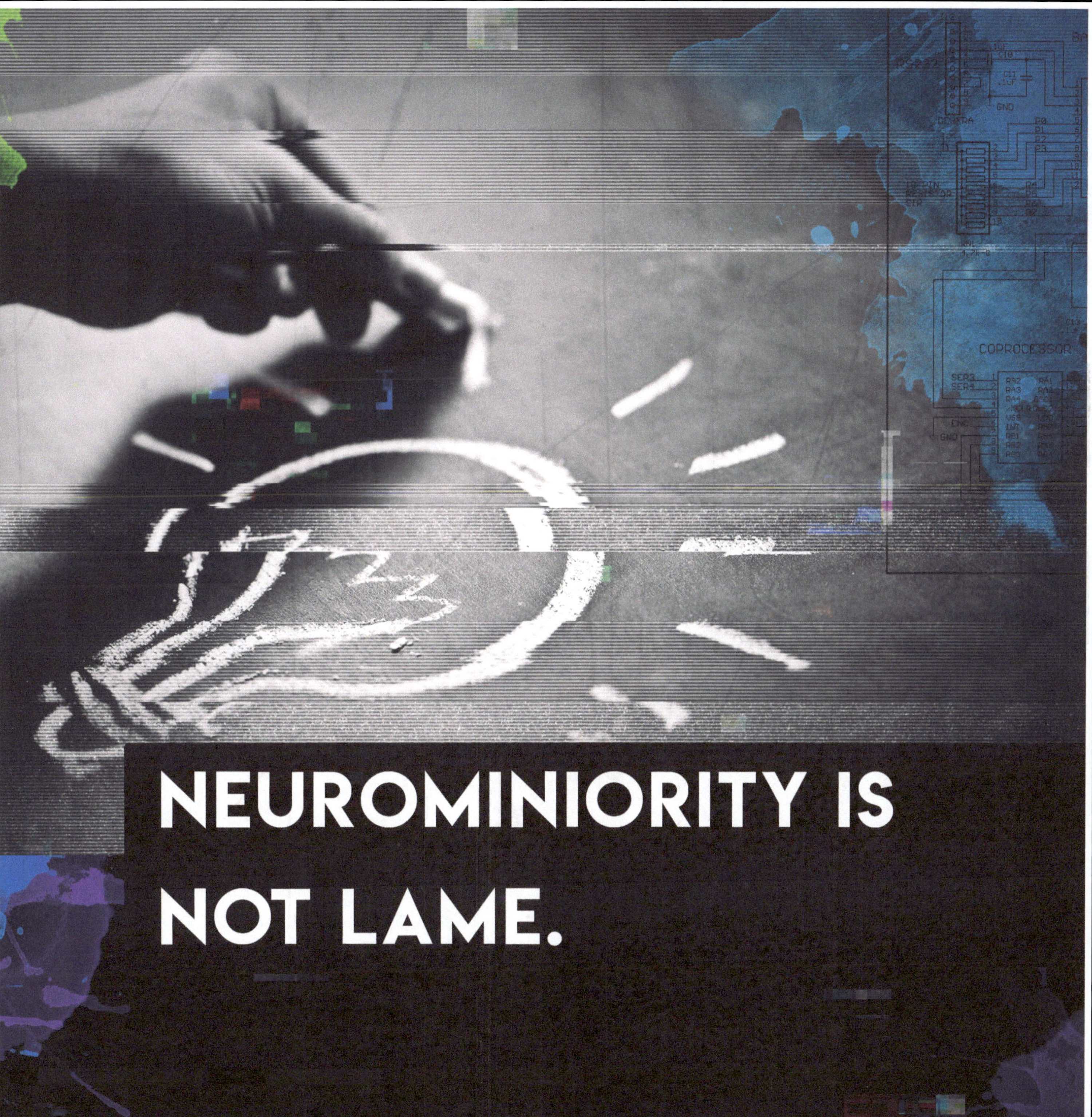

NEUROMINIORITY IS
NOT LAME.

I AM NORMAL
SO ARE YOU.

MY SHOES I WEAR
ARE NOT A FEW.

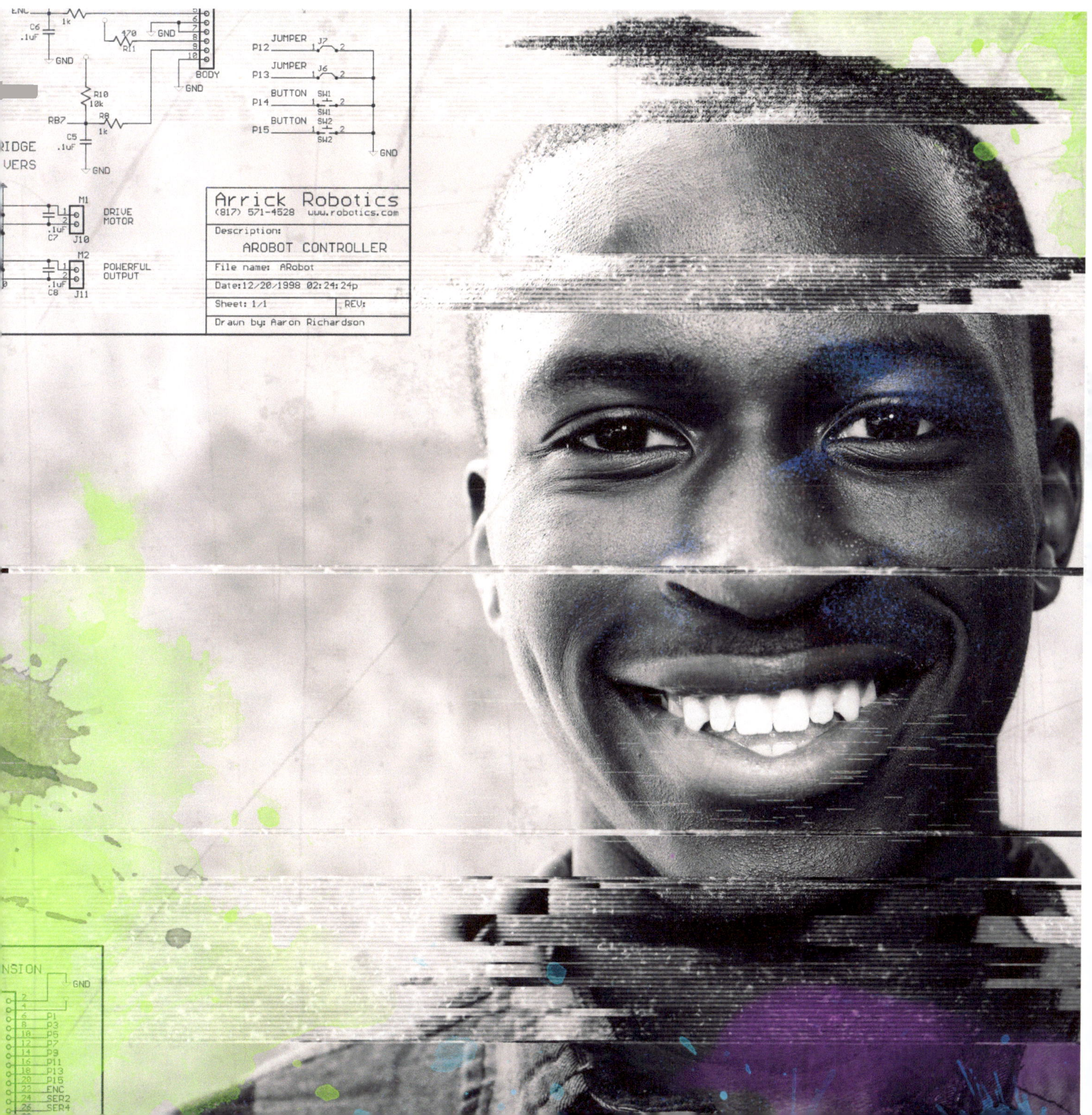
ENC
C6
.1uF
1k
GND
170
R11
GND
RB7
R10
10k
R9
1k
C5
.1uF
GND
BODY
GND
JUMPER
P12   J7
JUMPER   1   2
P13   J6
           1   2
BUTTON   SW1
P14   1   2
         SW1
BUTTON   SW2
P15   1   2
         SW2
GND
RIDGE
VERS
M1
L1
.1uF
C7   J10
DRIVE
MOTOR
M2
L1
.1uF
C8   J11
POWERFUL
OUTPUT
Arrick Robotics
(817) 571-4528   www.robotics.com
Description:
AROBOT CONTROLLER
File name: ARobot
Date:12/20/1998 02:24:24p
Sheet: 1/1   REV:
Drawn by: Aaron Richardson
NSION
GND
2
4
6   P1
8   P3
10   P5
12   P7
14   P9
16   P11
18   P13
20   P15
22   ENC
24   SER2
26   SER4

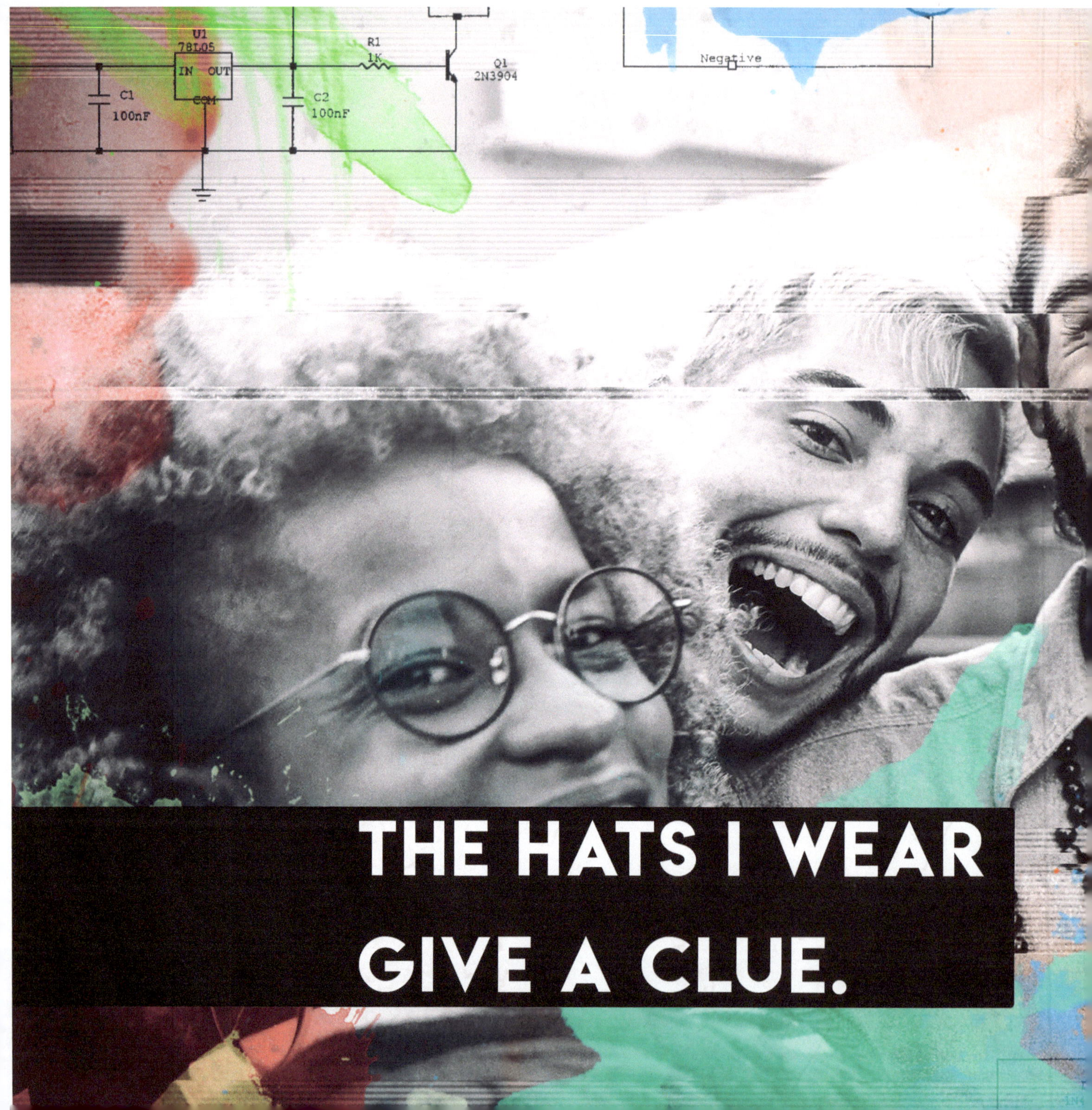
U1
78L05
IN OUT
COM
C1
100nF
R1
1K
C2
100nF
Q1
2N3904
Negative
THE HATS I WEAR
GIVE A CLUE.

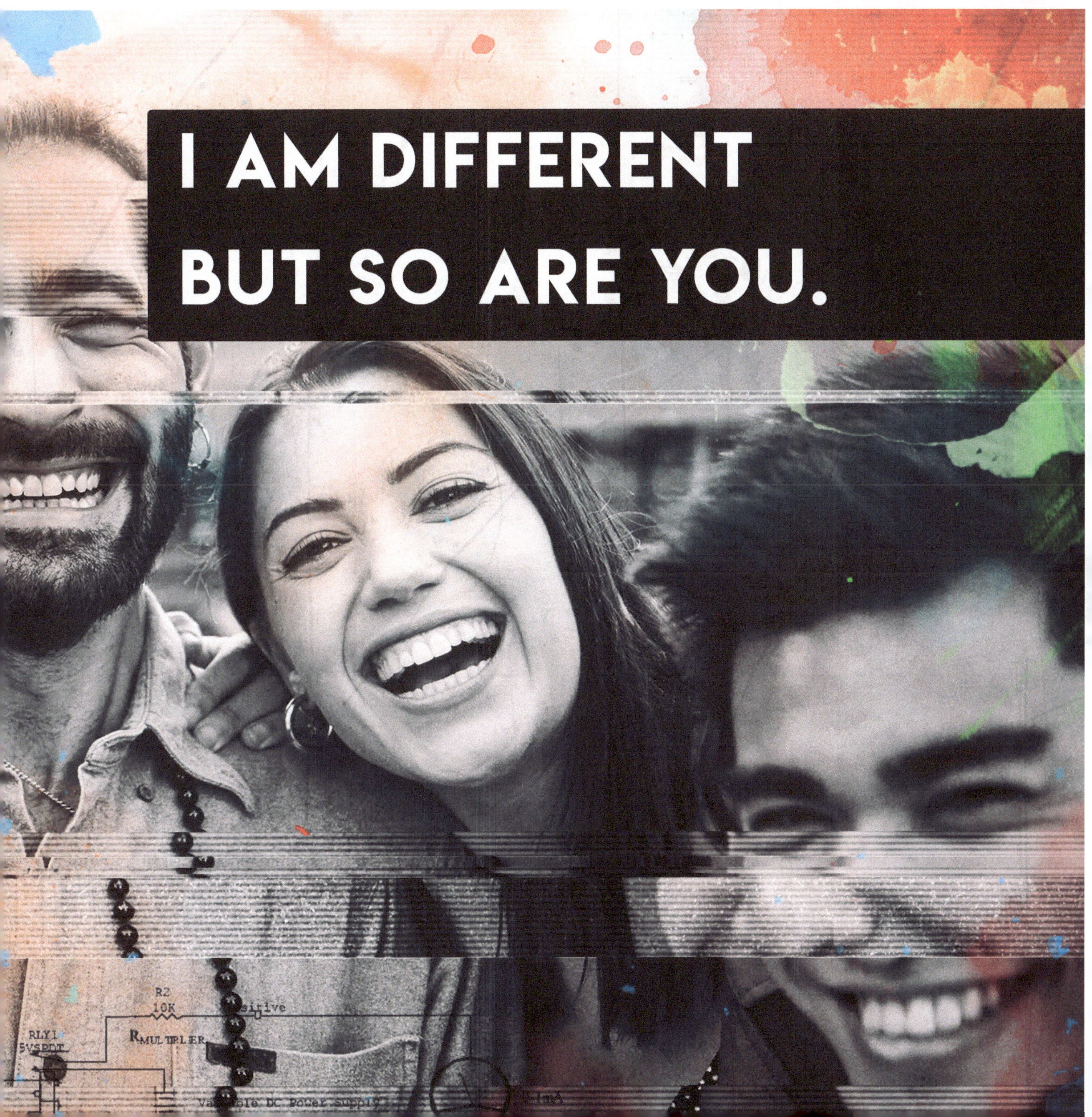

I AM DIFFERENT
BUT SO ARE YOU.